ADVANCED EVANGELISM

"A BIBLICAL WORLDVIEW"

PRYOR | BRIGGS

ADVANCED EVANGELISM
"A BIBLICAL WORLDVIEW"

Ginosko Media

ISBN-13: 978-0692572986 (Paperback)
ISBN-10: 0692572988

Subject Heading:
RELIGION | APOLOGETICS | DOCTRINAL THEOLOGY
First Edition

Printed in America

CONTENTS

Bookmarks

ACKNOWLEDGEMENTS

I would first like to thank my wife, LaToya Pryor, for allowing me the time and space to pursue academic and ministerial interests. For putting up with the books that covered the house a little longer than I had promised and a little more expansively than I had originally intended. Your support throughout the years have been immeasurable in my spiritual and scholastic life.

To Erick, Jr. and Emmanuel that you would engage the world with a worldview that declares Jesus Christ as LORD and Savior.

To my friend and business associate with Ginosko Media Publishing, Mr. Dedrick Briggs, for his friendship, consultation, and additional eyes, expertise, and excellence on the manuscript at various stages.

To my mother, Veronica Pryor, for her constant support. My sister, Rachel Rada, for her positive provocation throughout the years (yes, you are still smarter than me little sis!).

To my late father, Mr. Edward George Pryor, for his constant support within different endeavors of education, ministry, and writing. Though this isn't the book I had mentioned to him, I am sure he would be just as excited none the less.

To my Kingdom Life Academy and Community Outreach Reaching Everyone family at New Jerusalem Cathedral. May your efforts to spread the Gospel, empower your environment with the Word of God, and impact the world with principles gleaned from the kingdom of God be fruitful and influential. It is my prayer that this book may help you to stand unintimidated and sure in the faith and in the One who sent you for such a time as this.

~ **Dr. Erick G. Pryor, Sr.**

To my wonderful wife (LaToya A. Briggs), God designed you for me. I've come to appreciate our adversities because through them God taught us Love (1 John 4:8). I look forward to the rest of this life with you. May the beat of our hearts grow more in sync.

To my dear children, I often write that I might multiply my gifts in you. And in doing so, I lay this foundation that was not laid for me. Therefore, continue my evangelistic works, and be wholly committed to the Lord. For there is One God. One Savior. And His name is Jesus Christ. It is my earnest desire that you all take up arms and fight the good fight of faith. Put on your entire armor and prepare yourselves against the kingdom of darkness. Sharpen your swords daily and battle intelligently. For the cares of this world will pass away, but the principles of God's Word will always remain. Currently, you are still too young to hold a Sword. By then, I may be an old man, but I shall still be your affectionate father.

To my friend and brother of the faith (Erick G. Pryor), I could not ask for a more committed business partner and companion in the work of the Lord. Your friendship has been priceless.

To all of my fellow Fire Fighters throughout the city of Greensboro, NC, but especially to Andy, Brian, Preston and Jimmy, I truly believe the Lord brought us together.

Finally, to the churches of New Jerusalem Cathedral of whom I love. I thank God for you and mention you in my prayers. May grace and peace be with you all. May our words edify and burden you to boldly share the Gospel of our Lord and Savior Jesus Christ.

~ **Dedrick R. Briggs, Sr.**

INTRODUCTION

"But sanctify the Lord God in your hearts: and be ready always to give an answer to every man that asketh you a reason of the hope that is in you with meekness and fear: ^{16.} *Having a good conscience; that, whereas they speak evil of you, as of evildoers, they may be ashamed that falsely accuse your good conversation in Christ."*

~ 1 Peter 3:15-16

The Problem within Christianity

Today, many professing Christians seem to live in a bubble. When asked to publically declare their faith, they become fearful and reserved due to the possibility of being offensive or seen as a religious bigot for holding a view supported by the Bible. Hiding behind the four walls of their local assemblies and ignoring the responsibility to share the Gospel of Jesus Christ with love and compassion, such a Christian chooses their own comfort over the responsibility of being a disciple. The Christian bubble also allows them to ignore the sin in their own lives, along with the degraded moral condition of the world. Instead of being a part of the solution, many nominal Christians often ignore or criticize those who are doing their best to effectively share the Gospel of Jesus Christ. Through this resource, we intend to help Christians of all backgrounds become true disciples for the cause of Jesus Christ.

Fact

The largest and fastest growing religions according to the Pew Research Center are Islam and Christianity. Pew predicts that Islam, the world's fastest growing faith, will leap from 1.6 billion (in 2010) to 2.76 billion by 2050. At that time Muslims will make up nearly one-third of the world's total projected population of about 9 billion people. Christianity is expected to grow, too, but not at Islam's explosive rate.

The Pew study predicts Christians will increase from 2.17 billion to 2.92 billion, composing more than 31% of the world's population. This means that by 2050, more than 6 out of 10 people on Earth will be Christian or Muslim. And, for perhaps the first time in history, Islam and Christianity will be roughly equal in numbers.[1] However, despite the demographics of the Pew Research Center, we suspect that Islam is or will eventually become the world's dominate religion.

Why is this important? Matthew 24:14 states that the Gospel of the kingdom will be preached in all the world for a witness. If the Gospel is the power of God unto salvation, the fault is not in the gospel message, but in a lack of its proclamation. Remember that a tree is known by its fruit according to Matthew 12:33. So, what are we to think of a tree that produces no fruit? The fruit of the righteous is a tree of life; and he that winneth souls is wise (Proverbs 11:30). Because of this problem within Christianity, we would like to welcome the reader to the purpose of this book.

What is Truth?

"Truth no longer concerns the nature of things, nor is it subject to intellectual analysis."

~ **Douglas Groothius**

Introduction

Sir Francis Bacon is acknowledged for a quote in which he links the question of truth to the inquiry by Pontius Pilate to Jesus Christ. The interesting element of the inquiry, which Bacon points out, is that Pilate does not wait for the answer to his question of "what is truth?" Truth in our society is plagued by either oversimplification or hyper-complexity. A mere assertion to have truth or search for truth becomes more personal, subjective, and specifically categorized as to not invite in anyone else for scrutiny. So, what is truth? Is it merely something that we have constructed a compendium of facts for a particular viewpoint? Or could it be more?

When truth is spoken of in conversation, it is most likely referred to in the sense of objective truth. However, subjective truth is frequently inferred. The question of truth according to Groothius has two core components:

1. What is the nature of truth itself?
2. What does it mean for something (i.e. a belief or statement) to be true as opposed to false, or simply nonsense?[2]

The Question of Truth

This section opened with Francis Bacon's examination into the question of Pontius Pilate. Pilate's question of, *"What is truth?"*, still intrigues us today in our age of ubiquitous information, research, and academic expertise. Engaging in the question of truth in our 21st century brings to light the Christian claim to exclusivity. Christians, adhering to the standard of the Scriptures, hold to the principle that Jesus Christ is the only way. Other religions and those that ascribe to the belief that there is no God, hold the position that it is impossible for the Christian to make such a claim. Questions pertaining to the truth of such a position arise such as, "How can the Christian faith claim it is the exclusive worldview?" or "Has the Christian studied every religion in order to substantiate their claims for exclusivity?" These questions hinge on the principles we use to build a concept of truth.

Therefore, it must be stated that all beliefs, whether religious or secular, claim some level of exclusivity. As much as one may attempt to claim tolerance and inclusion, there is still a point of exclusion. No worldview survives without its own distinct element of being in the world. Truth, if it is to be identified as such, cannot consist of subjective truths. There must be principles that define even "little" truths, "a" truth or one's personal truths. These are the principles that will be discussed throughout this book.

Have you studied all Religions?

A religion (worldview) is how someone views or thinks about the world. It is how we look at the world and how we make sense of that world. Worldviews have been compared to a lens that we look through, but do not see.[3] Our judgments, our actions, and our ideas are governed by the worldview we hold. Leo Apostol is credited for his work on worldview analysis in describing a worldview as a descriptive model of the world with several elements.[4] Apostol's worldview analysis consisted of:

1. An explanation of the world
2. An answer to the future of the world
3. A method or theory of action;
4. A theory of knowledge
5. Lastly, an account of the building blocks of your worldview

Apostol's contribution also consisted of six questions to accompany these elements of a worldview: How do we explain the world? Where are we heading? What should we do? How should we attain our goals?

Introduction

What is true and false? What is the origin and construction of our worldview?[5] With these questions we can appropriately "see the lens" that we look through when viewing the world.

It is believed that there are as many religions as there are people today. Yet, the majority of Christians know very little of the major religions of the world. Fortunately, the vast majority of religions can be classified within these three religious worldviews:

Monotheism	Polytheism	Pantheism
The word monotheism comes from the Greek *monos*, which means one, and *theos*, which means god. Hence, monotheism is a belief in the existence of one God. This view is equivalent to the potter (Creator) and the clay (Creation).	The term polytheism is based on the Greek roots *poly*, which means many, and *theos*, which means god. Hence, a variety of gods are acknowledged and/or worshipped.	Pantheism is either the belief that the universe is God or the sum total of all that exist. Therefore, God is whomever you regard him to be. This sort of view can be seen within eastern religions like Hinduism, and the "New Age" philosophies.

Non-religious worldviews include *Atheism* (the belief that there is no God) and *Agnosticism* (the uncertainty of the existence of God). These categorical themes help to simplify the process of classifying all systems of belief. Although categorization is simple, these worldviews remain vastly different.

"The foundation to proper apologetics is salvation and spiritual maturity, critical thinking skills, and sound theology."

~ Ryan Turner

What is Apologetics?

You don't need a doctorate in Theology or Biblical Studies to be an effective apologist. Within apologetics, we attempt to make a defense for our Biblical faith. Any act of sharing the Bible is operating within Christian apologetics. In fact, we are commanded to be apologist by Jesus himself: "And he said unto them, Go ye into all the world, and preach the gospel to every creature." (Mark 16:15). If God commands us to preach, then we must make a defense. "But sanctify the Lord God in your hearts: and be ready always to give an answer to every man that asketh you a reason of the hope that is in you with meekness and fear:" (1 Pet.3:15).

The context of the word *answer* originates from the Greek word ἀπολογια. The transliteration of this term is **apologia** (ap-ol-og-ee'-ah) meaning a verbal defense, speech in defense of, or a reasoned statement or argument. Thus, apologetics is an element within Christianity that deals with the defense and proclamation of the gospel of Jesus Christ.

Every true believer should be involved in apologetics based upon what has been modeled by Jesus throughout the Gospels. When you become a Christian, you are automatically assigned to be an apologist. As a result, all Christians are called to be apologists. For many Christians, the reality of Apologetics is dreadful, but Jesus is with you. As you equip yourself through in-depth studying, prayer, and fasting, the Lord will work through you within your individual capacity (Rom. 12:3; 2 Cor. 10:15).

Introduction

What is "Hate Speech"?

Hateful speech is something that all Christians should avoid. The term "Hate speech," is often used by secular thinkers to attack or derail Christians from their assignments. Anything that does not coincide with the secular perspective is usually branded as hate speech. According to dictionary.com, hate speech is, "speech that attacks a person or group on the basis of race, religion, gender, or sexual orientation." The deception within this definition is the inclusion of religion and sexual orientation because they are changeable and can be influenced by fundamental truths or one's emotional state. However, one's ethnicity and gender are unchangeable and sacred aspects of their God-given identity. Methods that intend to assassinate another person's identity or reputation is true hate speech. Therefore, hate speech is speech intended to degrade, intimidate, or incite violence or prejudicial action against one's sacred identity based on race, ethnicity, national origin, or disability. Biblical Evangelism is that which denounces anything that profanes the relevance and truth of the Bible as it pertains to humanity. One's religion, sexual orientation, and immoral contemplations or decisions can be denounced without attacking the sacredness of another's identity. Hate speech is the attack of one's sacred identity, which is never acceptable and should never be tolerated among Bible-believing Christians.

Conversely, as Christians, we have the same right to freely speak about our faith as those who exercise their right to label us homophobes, bigots, and hate-mongers. Equally, in labeling us, they commit the exact offense by which they accuse us (Matt. 9:24; Mar. 5:40; Luke 8:53). Therefore, the mockery of the secular mind should not deter the Christian from sharing the message of the gospel of Jesus Christ. As proud Christians, we should rejoice when we are persecuted considering Christ was also unjustly persecuted (1 Cor.

2:8). We must bless those who persecute us (Rom. 12:14), but this does not mean that we do not have the right to defend ourselves (Luke 22:36). Moreover, we should never return evil for evil. In fact, whenever possible, we are to pursue peace with all (Rom. 12:17-18).

Therefore, it is not bigotry or hate speech to profess that immorality (i.e. rape, pedophilia, incest, homosexuality, pornography, adultery, cheating, lying, etc.) is wrong according to the Bible. The greatest defeat within Christianity is not death. The greatest defeat among Christians occurs when they allow secular thinkers to muzzle or censor their proclamation of the Gospel of Jesus Christ.

The Purpose of this Book

Aside from what the general populous learns from the mainstream media, family and friends, or from listening to the preacher on Sunday mornings at church; if all professing Christians were probed about the more in-depth tenets of the Bible or the above religious demographics, the majority of them would not know.

The purpose of this book is to educate the general public of the history, doctrines, and differences in various major or influential religions. Since core beliefs influence one's ethical decision making, we have also included a section addressing key ethical issues facing our world today. This supplemental resource serves as a call to all Christians to properly equip themselves and begin aggressively sharing the Gospel message of Jesus Christ intelligently and empathetically.

Another purpose of this resource is to dispute any notion that in-depth study is strictly for preachers and not for laypersons. Voddie Baucham, a Baptist minister from Houston, Texas, believes we have a phenomenon in the church that is not found anywhere else. He gives the example of a man working a skilled trade for twenty years and being approached by a new worker and asking to be mentored. It is expected that the man with such experience will be able to mentor the

Introduction

new worker in the skilled trade successfully. Unfortunately, we have many people in the church with a similar amount of time, but they are not expected to have knowledge of doctrine, history, theology, and bible study methods necessary to adequately mentor. Oftentimes, we refer people wanting mentorship to those with a title. This should not be the case.

"And he said unto them, Go ye into all the world, and preach the gospel to every creature."

~ Mark 16:15

The last words of Christ to those that believe in Him were to go into the world and preach the gospel. Though the words sound simple enough, only two percent of all admitted Christians share their faith to those that do not believe. The excuses for not following this last earthly command are many, but ultimately as a Bible believing Christian one is obligated to share the saving knowledge of the gospel.

Saved and unsaved have memorized John 3:16, and feel they understand its meaning. God so loves that He gave His son at Calvary. All man has to do is believe in Him and everlasting life is granted as a result. In response, man feels that he has a free pass to sin without obligation, responsibility or any concern for judgment. This is not the saving knowledge of the gospel the Christian is to present, but often this is what the world gets.

The content of this book is to address the proper conception of salvation and develop a scriptural basis for what is commonly termed, "being saved." In so doing, the pages of this book will also present a scriptural basis for what is commonly referred to as "soul winning." Other definitions will also be defined scripturally as they will be used throughout the book such as sin, grace, and salvation for further clarity on what the last words of Christ say to believers everywhere.

Every Bible believing Christian is an Apologist, which is someone who defends the Gospel. As a Christian Apologist, it is important that you become sharper at critical thinking. Next, it's important to accurately define the term Worldview. According to James W. Sire, a worldview is, "a commitment, a fundamental orientation of the heart, that can be expressed as a story or in a set of presuppositions (assumptions which may be true, partially true or entirely false) that we hold (consciously or subconsciously, consistently or inconsistently) about the basic constitution of reality, and that provides the foundation on which we live and move and have our being." F. Leroy Forlines defines it a little more explicitly by saying, "…a worldview is simply the total set of beliefs that a person has about the biggest questions in life." Ken Ham, CEO of Answers in Genesis, had this to say about the term *worldview*: *"What you believe about who you are, where you came from, affects your whole worldview."*

This resource is presented with the hope that you will be encouraged to study more deeply with correct methods of inquiry into the Word of God. We are all responsible for building up the body of Christ, from the preacher to the layperson. Just as Nehemiah built the wall with the aid of others who focused on their particular section, the church must do the same. Study this document, share it, and be encouraged to investigate God's Word.

Notes

CHAPTER 1

"YOU MUST BE BORN AGAIN"

There are various clichés and trite phrases within American Christianity that make understanding difficult. Adding to this difficulty is the fact that most do not know the definition of these terms that are all too frequently used by most or all. One such term is that of "born again." Believers or simple readers of the Bible are introduced to this term in the Gospel of John in the third chapter of the book. Here one is introduced to the concept by the Master Teacher Himself, Jesus Christ.

An Introduction to Nicodemus

John 3 opens with an introduction to a man named Nicodemus. Nicodemus was a Pharisee. According to the Apostle Paul, a Pharisee was of the strictest sects of the Jews (Philippians 3). During the three and a half years that Jesus engaged in ministry,

Pharisees were some of His most fierce opponents. The record of
John changes our perception of the Pharisees as a whole with the
introduction of this man who comes to Jesus at night to ask him
questions. Nicodemus opens with a declaration of who he
understands motivates and empowers the activity of Jesus:

*"[T]he same came to Jesus by night, and said unto him, Rabbi, we know that
thou art a teacher come from God: for no man can do these miracles that thou
doest, except God be with him."*

~ **John 3:2**

Nicodemus understood that Jesus was sent by God and this was the
impetus of His miracles. Jesus responds to Nicodemus by saying that
he must be born again to see the kingdom of God. The response to
Nicodemus is a response to us all. Regardless of our religious piety,
our sin, or our fiscal status in life, we must be born again or as Jesus
explains in the original language, born from above or born of the
Spirit.

This chapter will explain Jesus's conversation with Nicodemus
in order to discuss the concept and principles concerning how we
must be born again. Using John chapter 3 as a backdrop, we will
explore the differences between flesh and spirit and the necessity of
the soul being saved from the consequences of man's sin and God's
impending wrath for this sin.

That Which is Born of Flesh is Flesh

"That which is born of the flesh is flesh; and that which is
born of the Spirit is spirit. Marvel not that I said unto thee, Ye must
be born again. The wind bloweth where it listeth, and thou hearest the
sound thereof, but canst not tell whence it cometh, and whither it
goeth: so is every one that is born of the Spirit" (John 3:6-8). The

Greek word for flesh is *sarkikos*. This word is representative of the natural state of men and women, the base nature of man, and the character associated with the fallen status of man. In Genesis 2:7, we read, "And the LORD God formed man *of* the dust of the ground, and breathed into his nostrils the breath of life; and man became a living soul" (Genesis 2:7).

Man is formed, breathed into, and became at the hands and breath of God. This act of creation gave man a body, spirit, and soul, respectively. John 3 does not discuss the soul, but exclusively highlights the body and spirit. Jesus's talk with Nicodemus focused on the component not mentioned, the soul. When we are born, we are birthed as a living soul. In the womb, a body forms, spirit or animation is present as a child in the womb kicks and squirms as it grows, but the personality, the mind, emotion, and capacity is dormant within the soul. It is the soul that we mourn in death, not the body. It is the soul that dreams and envisions things. And thus this same soul has the ability to affirm or deny Jesus Christ as Lord through the vehicle of the will.

What the creation and the fall of man both show us is that God had a purpose and plan in mind for man. Dr. Myles Munroe, often called the apostle of purpose, defines purpose as the original intent or design of a thing. The original purpose of man was to operate in the image and likeness of their Creator in an optimal environment where a body of work has been designated. When man fell, the optimal environment was no longer available for him to work in. Also, his will was tarnished by a mind that sought to operate contrary to the original purpose for which he was created. The aftermath of the fall was operation solely within the vehicle and motivation of the flesh. Next, we examine the works of the flesh that emerged from this new emphasis on carnality or fleshly things.

The Works of the Flesh (Galatians 5)

Scripture says that the flesh "lusts" after the Spirit (Gal. 5:17). God's design is that the Spirit of God speaks to your spirit and directs your soul, which in turn directs your body or flesh. The flesh would like the position that the Spirit should occupy in your life. The flesh "desires illegally" (lusts) after the position that it was never supposed to occupy. When this occurs, the flesh produces after the baseness of its nature and desires. Galatians 5:19-21, defines this list of what the flesh produces as the works of the flesh. Paul says that the works of the flesh are manifested through adultery, fornication, uncleanness, lasciviousness, idolatry, witchcraft, hatred, variance, emulations, wrath, strife, seditions, heresies, envyings, murders, drunkenness, and revellings.

Notice that the works of the flesh result in the main idea of Christ's words in John 3:5, Jesus answered, "Verily, verily, I say unto thee, Except a man be born of water and *of* the Spirit, he cannot enter into the kingdom of God." There is no entrance or inheritance, literally to come into existence and to receive, without first being "born" and "walking" in the Spirit of God. The works of the flesh are a natural inclination for everyone. As vile as the different depictions of the works of the flesh sound, it is necessary for men and women to fully embrace the kingdom of God.

The Fruit of the Spirit (Galatians 5)

In contrast, the fruit of the Spirit [of God] is love, joy, peace, longsuffering, gentleness, goodness, faith, meekness, temperance: against such there is no law. And they that are Christ's have crucified the flesh with the affections and lusts. If we live in the Spirit, let us also walk in the Spirit (Galatians 5:22-24).

The opposition of the flesh is not additional works, but fruit.

Fruit is an important look into the heart of God and His kingdom. If we have works, we have something that may still be motivated by the flesh, but having fruit is more impactful and showcases the manner of the individual. Recall, that Jesus said, "Either make the tree good, and his fruit good; or else make the tree corrupt, and his fruit corrupt: for the tree is known by *his* fruit" (Matthew 12:33).

Notice Jesus focuses on the tree. A tree is something established and often is used scripturally to symbolize a leader (recall Daniel 4 and the dream of Nebuchadnezzar). Trees are established by fruit not leaves, not branches, and not how they cover in Summer or showcase color in the Fall. In the same way fruit is the currency of the Spirit-filled life.

A Son of God?

"And as Moses lifted up the serpent in the wilderness, even so must the Son of man be lifted up: that whosoever believeth in him should not perish, but have eternal life. For God so loved the world, that he gave his only begotten Son, that whosoever believeth in him should not perish, but have everlasting life" (John 3:14-16).

John 3:16 is a very common verse and is quoted by saved and unsaved alike. God sent His Son in order for those that believe on Him might be saved. Jesus's death, burial, and resurrection was the culmination of an integrated system that spread throughout the Old Testament law and the prophets.

Being Born Again?

"Marvel not that I said unto thee, Ye must be born again" (John 3:7). Vine's Expository Dictionary of New Testament Words states the word born (Greek *gennao*), especially in the writings of the Apostle John, speaks of the gracious act of God in conferring upon those who

believe the nature and disposition of "children," imparting to them spiritual life.

Just like we are born along the natural plane, we must be "born again" into the spiritual life. David in the Psalms states that he was "shapen in iniquity," and "conceived" in "sin" (Psalm 51:5). The fallen nature of Adam transfers to us and is explicitly revealed in Scripture (Romans 5:12). Adam's sin passed to us and we therefore are granted the wages of that sin and death (Romans 6:23). However, we must understand what is meant by death. God told Adam in Eden that in the day that he ate of the tree of knowledge of good and evil he would "surely die" (Genesis 2:17). Yet, upon the eating of the fruit of the tree, Adam and his wife did not fall down dead at that moment. So, is the Bible wrong? Let's look at Genesis 2:16-17 regarding what death is according to the Bible:

"And the LORD God commanded the man, saying, Of every tree of the garden thou mayest freely eat: but of the tree of the knowledge of good and evil, thou shalt not eat of it: for in the day that thou eatest thereof thou shalt surely die."

Here the word *die* is the Hebrew word *muwth*, meaning to be killed or put to death. Nothing exceptional here. But considering the full Biblical record, namely Genesis and the situation here with Adam being told in the day he ate he would die, we understand death is potentially something more than when a physical body is lifeless. Note Revelation 20:12:

"And I saw the dead, small and great, stand before God; and the books were opened: and another book was opened, which is the book of life: and the dead were judged out of those things which were written in the books, according to their works."

If these individuals are dead, how are they standing and how are the dead judged. Dead here is the Greek word *nekros* meaning lifeless or one whose soul has departed. A body void of the soul is said to be a "dead" body. The soul away from the body is a soul separated from the body. Therefore, we see death is a type of separation. We understand it best as a physical separation of the soul from the body. Saying that we are spiritually born could also mean that we can be spiritually dead. If someone is spiritually dead, they are separated from the spiritual life that God provides. When Adam died initially, it was a separation from the life he once knew in Eden and with accessibility to the presence of God.

For this cause, Jesus says that unless we are born again, we cannot see or enter the kingdom of God. In John 3:3, the word for see is *eido* meaning to perceive or be attentive to in order to experience. We do not experience all that God has desired for us without being born again. Not being born again in this life results in our being disqualified from experiencing the kingdom of God beyond our physical death. This is why Christ died and why His conversation with Nicodemus took the turn it did to discover the essence of being born again. It explains why the son of Man would be lifted up, even as the serpent was in the wilderness (John 3:14; Numbers 21:7-9).

The Baptism of the Holy Spirit

To better grasp what it means to be born again, we also have to understand the Baptism of the Holy Spirit. This phenomenon was unheard of until the time of John the Baptist. The first mention of the Holy Spirit operating within the lives of people was initially declared in the gospels by John the Baptist.

Here we must answer a fundamental question, "What is the baptism of the Holy Spirit?" The baptism of the Holy Spirit comes directly from Jesus. John the Baptist said, "He that cometh after me is mightier than I, whose shoes I am not worthy to bear: he shall baptize you with the Holy Ghost, and with fire" (Matthew 3:11). The baptism of the Holy Spirit is a critical element within the Christian faith because it is the confirmation of the indwelling of the Spirit of God Himself. Not only is it important, it is a gift from God. This indwelling of the Spirit of God helps to guide the individual in daily life, along with what most would consider trivial. It is also important for believers to understand the necessity of the Holy Spirit. Prior to His ascension Jesus said, "But ye shall receive power, after that the Holy Ghost is come upon you: and ye shall be witnesses unto me both in Jerusalem, and in all Judaea, and in Samaria, and unto the uttermost part of the earth" (Acts 1:8). The risen Jesus instructed the apostles to wait in Jerusalem for the coming of the Holy Spirit. Prior to His ascension, He commissioned them for a world-wide mission and promised that they would be empowered for this by the Holy Spirit."[6] According to an article published by the Christian Broadcast Network, "The baptism in the Holy Spirit is an empowering for service that takes place in the life of the Christian (Acts 1:5, 8). In it we are immersed in the Spirit's life and power."[7]

The Person of the Holy Spirit?

Many people speak of the Holy Spirit as some sort of allegorical concept. Many refer to the Holy Spirit as an "it" instead of a literal person from the triune being of God. Of all the spiritual endowments imparted by God within humanity, the greatest of all is the assignment of the Holy Spirit within the lives of His believers. The Holy Spirit has many functions in the life of the believer, but the first of them is that He works in the hearts of all that receive Him. Jesus told His followers that He would send the Comforter (Holy Spirit) into the world to "convict the world in regards to sin, righteousness, and judgment" (John 16:7-11). Consider the words of John F.

Walvoord when he stated, *"It may be noted that the Holy Spirit possesses the essential of mind or intelligence. The Scriptures explicitly affirm that the Holy Spirit exercises a moral and sovereign will comparable to that of the other Persons of the Trinity. In connection with the sovereign bestowal of spiritual gifts on men, the Spirit is said to accomplish this "as he will"* (1 Cor. 12:11). *The essential of mind or intelligence is further confirmed by His works. His works indicate intelligence, knowledge, and the normal functions of personality. Personality, which is an attribute of His Person, is demonstrated by the actions of the Person. The attributes of omniscience is evidence of the existence of mind and intelligence on a plane of deity"* (1 Cor. 2:10-11).[8]

Notes

CHAPTER 2

"SIN, THE LAW, & REPENTANCE"

Throughout the scriptures there is clear indication on God's view of sin. God established His law to mankind and lets man know that he will be judged by His expectation for His conduct. The effects of sin are so far reaching that it took the sacrifice of Christ to erase the effect this contaminant had on mankind (Romans 5:12-14).

Sin

"What shall we say then? Shall we continue in sin, that grace may abound? God forbid. How shall we, that are dead to sin, live any longer therein?"

~ Romans 6:1-2

According to scripture, sin entered the world through Adam and simultaneously death entered and passed upon all. But what is sin as it is stated in these scriptures? The word sin used in Romans 5 and other passages in the New Testament means to "miss the mark as to not share in the prize." Sin is a governing principle or power and finds its end in acts of disobedience to divine law.[9] If an individual gives into sin they miss the standard that the divine law has set up for them. For this reason, those that do not have a relationship with Jesus Christ are referred to as the lost (Matthew 18:10; Luke 19:11). Lost is to be in an active state of perishing or destruction, which is sin's aim (Romans 6:23).

Sin's hold on mankind is not external, but has man within the very heart of his being controlling him at his core.[10] Therefore, man cannot escape sin and its effects. No remedy is within the boundaries of earth to relieve man of the pressures of sin. Ultimately, the principle of sin applies pressure on man until it achieves its end to not only rule, but to bring death upon man (James 1:14-15).

The Law

"Wherefore the law was our schoolmaster to bring us unto Christ, that we might be justified by faith. But after that faith is come, we are no longer under a schoolmaster."

~ Galatians 3:24-25

Romans 5:14 states that death reigned or had governing power from Adam to Moses. Literally, there was no remedy to the effects of sin. Subsequently, sin reigned or ruled over all human life without remedy. From Adam to Moses denotes the element of law that was instituted. The law teaches what sin is and creates sin for man. This is important since in identifying what sin is, man can then distinguish when he is going astray, know what is in opposition to the law, and can make a free-will decision to abide by the law or not (Romans 7:7-8). The law is extremely important in the conversion of the soul to Christ. Paul states in Romans 7:8, "without the law sin was dead."

Dead in this context means inanimate, inactive and destitute of force or power. Where there is no law, there is no knowledge of sin (Romans 3:20).

The law spoken of here and in other verses throughout the New Testament is the Law of Moses. Mosaic Law is detailed concisely in Exodus. From this succinct depiction of God's law, man can see the 613 laws that comprised the full law. James 2:19 stated that an individual that broke one of the laws was guilty of breaking all of them. Therefore it is easy to see that the end result of trying to keep the law fully was death due to the impossibility of man keeping all 613 commandments without error (*Exodus 20:3-17; Galatians 3:24-25*).

There was a purpose in the law of God. Scripture indicates that it was a schoolmaster, instructor, or guardian. In Paul's time, the schoolmaster was an individual in a Greek household that took management over a boy of seven years of age until eighteen years of age and insured that he got to school safely, conducted himself appropriately outside the home, and teaches him proper morals and manners.[11] The law therefore was to take charge of an individual to guide them into maturity, which in this case is justification by faith. However, this justification requires an acknowledgement of wrongdoing and further a turn from such wrongdoing.

Repentance

"I say unto you, that likewise joy shall be in heaven over one sinner that repenteth, more than over ninety and nine just persons, which need no repentance."

~ **Luke 15:7**

God is patient towards man and does not want mankind to be destroyed. However, man must comply with the terms that God has established. God has established freedom from the dominating power of sin and death through repentance (2 Peter 3:9). Repentance means to change one's mind or purpose. Many mistake changing the mind as just a flippant gesture requiring no action, yet true repentance means a turn in the opposite direction of past actions. Scripture details God's view of repentance very clearly (Romans 2:4).

Many state that God is a good and loving God and therefore, would not send anyone to hell. This is not true based on the scriptural representation of God's nature and expectations for mankind. Repentance is an essential element to belief in Christ and cannot be overlooked. Many risk not truly reaping the benefits of salvation due to lack of repentance. The Bible is very clear that God has less interest in our material offerings, but a broken and repentant heart (Ps. 51:16-19; 2 Cor. 7:10; Eph. 2:8-9).

Looking at the words of King David in Psalm 51, one can see what God looks for. God does not desire works, but true repentance. Your works do not save you; it is the condition of your heart. God is looking for right standing with Him, which ultimately begins with understanding how you match up in comparison to God's law. Understanding the role of sin and how man has sinned against the perfect law of God, he has understanding of God's law and is aware of his need to repent *(Deuteronomy 32:4; Psalms 19:7).*

CHAPTER 3

"SALVATION"

"But the salvation of the righteous is of the LORD: he is their strength in the time of trouble."

~ Psalms 37:39

In order to be a Christian, you must be saved. Saved means you have accepted the terms of salvation. Use of the words saved and salvation automatically bring up questions. What does it mean to be saved? What is salvation? How does one achieve this end? For the purpose of clarification it is necessary to define and properly apply the terms used for salvation and saved in their original languages.

Salvation Terms in the Old Testament

There are five Hebrew terms in the Old Testament (OT) of the Bible defined as salvation. These terms are yeshuah, yasha, yesha, moshaah and teshuah. Each adds further insight into the concept of salvation while keeping a basic, fundamental concept of salvation.

1. **Yeshuah** is the most common term for salvation in the OT. It simply means something saved; deliverance; aid; victory; prosperity; health and welfare (Ex. 14:13; 2 Chr. 20:17; Ps. 119:155). The term yeshuah as used in the scriptures above illustrate some of the terms used in the definition. Moses and the children of Israel were commanded to wait on the LORD in Exodus 14:13. In so doing they as a people saw their deliverance from the Egyptians. God also secured a victory for them without any effort from them and His intervention caused them to be something saved.

2. **Yasha** and **yesha** are two similar terms for salvation used in the OT. However, yesha is more common and is derived from yasha, so it will be presented here. Yesha comes from the concept of yasha, which means to be open, wide or free. This term implies safety or being freed (rescue). Yesha means liberty, deliverance, or prosperity (Psalms 51:12; 1 Chr. 16:35).

3. **Moshaah** is also derived from yesha and means deliverance. Psalm 68:20 illustrates the use of this term. This particular scripture details worship towards God for His power to deliver from death (Psalms 68:20).

4. **Teshuah** is the last term used in the OT. This term describes rescue, deliverance, help, safety and victory. Once again this term is derived from yasha (Psalms 37:39, 38:22, 51:14, 50:23; Isa. 46:13)

Putting all of the terms together in a unified definition gives the understanding that salvation is the occurrence of something obtaining salvation; deliverance; aid; victory; prosperity; health and welfare. When an individual is a recipient of salvation they are open, wide or free from danger due to safety or being freed (rescue) from something binding. Ultimately, the individual receiving salvation finds liberty in what or who has bestowed this salvation.

Salvation Terms in the New Testament

The strength of what modern Christianity defines as salvation or being saved is expressed within the pages of the New Testament (NT). OT scriptures give the shadow of salvation, while the New Testament reveals the true nature of salvation. From studying the NT text, it is found that salvation is not an act or occurrence at all, but a person, Jesus Christ (Romans 1:16).

In order to appreciate the words of the Apostle Paul to the Romans it is essential to examine the NT words used for salvation and saved. Unlike the OT, there are only two words for these terms, *soteria* and *sozo*.

1. *Soteria* is the term often rendered salvation and *sozo*, the term for save. *Soteria* is a Greek word which means rescue or safety. Its use in classical Greek literature denotes preservation and was also a picture of an individual who had safely returned to his original country and home after an absence.[12] With this understanding the recipient of salvation is therefore one granted rescue from sin and its effects and the safety of not having to enter back into the binding constraints of a fallen world infected with sin. It through salvation that we are "saved" from the spiritual consequences of sin and the pollution of sin (Luke 1:77; Acts 4:12; Rom. 1:16, 10:10, 13:11; 2 Cor. 6:2, 7:10, 1 Thess. 5:9; 2 Tim. 3:15; Tit. 2:11; Heb. 2:3, 5:9, 9:28; 1 Pet. 1:9).[13]

2. *Sozo* is a Greek word meaning to save, deliver, make whole

or to preserve safe from danger, loss, and destruction. NT scripture uses *sozo* extensively within its definition. Scriptures using the term detail everything from deliverance of demonic spirits (Luke 8:36), healing from disease (Matthew 9:22), and eternal security through salvation (Acts 16:30-31)

Biblical Salvation

With the definition of both OT and NT words for saved and salvation, it is necessary to define scripturally what it means to be saved. As mentioned previously, salvation is not just an act or occurrence, it is a person. At Christ's birth, the name Jesus is given in confirmation of this fact (Matt. 1:21; 1 Cor. 1:30).

God has made Christ our wisdom, our basis for right standing with Him, a means of holiness as He is holy, and the redeeming factor back to Him. His name literally means the "LORD is salvation". He is salvation and the only means by which man can have right standing with God the Father (Matt. 18:11; John 3:17, 12:47).

Knowing that Jesus Christ is the sole source of salvation from sin and its effects (death), it is vital that one knows how to become saved or how to lead another to Christ. Take for example a simple analogy. An individual is swimming in the ocean. At first all is calm and the person enjoys being in the water and becomes comfortable enough to go further out. As the day presses on the individual realizes that what was once fun to be immersed in is now a threat to their safety, in fact if they are becoming tired and if they do not get out of the water they will inevitably drown. Without strength to swim to safety they cry out. In response, a lifeguard comes to their rescue. Obviously, the lifeguard is there to rescue the individual that "lost" his or her way, but the person must accept the help of the lifeguard by simply taking the help and submitting to the strength, expertise, and direction the lifeguard is taking them. You are the life guard. With this analogy as a model scriptures will be presented to illustrate how an individual receives the gift of salvation (Eph. 2:8).

First, understand that the individual drowning does not have the power within him to reach safety. Because he is immersed in something bigger than himself, struggling will only make him more tired and he will sink further. In the same way, all mankind is immersed in sin. It engulfs the nature of man until his only way out of it is Christ (Rom. 10:9, 13).

The swimmer must first admit that he needs help. With this confession is a verbal expression of his need for rescue. After this confession is made he must not doubt the ability of the one providing rescue since to do so means that he would not be led to a place of safety. One who calls upon Christ for rescue can be assured that their call for help is met with the Lord's promise of salvation (2 Pet. 3:9).

Adding further to this illustration is the fact that all men are drawn into the water of sin although all cannot swim within it and survive. All are drawn by desire for its contents even though its end is to kill man. God has provided redemption through Christ Jesus, but man must accept it. In so doing, man accepts rescue, security, liberty, deliverance, healing and restoration from sin and its consequences (Titus 3:5).

We will not be hasty to assume that everyone reading this book has accepted Jesus Christ as their personal Lord and Savior. Therefore, after reading this section, if you are not a Christian and want to be a follower of Jesus Christ, you can do so now. "Whoever will call on the name of the LORD shall be saved" (Romans 10:13). Your personal relationship with the Lord can begin right now through a sincere and repentant heart, and open confession through simple prayers like:

Salvation

"Heavenly Father, please forgive me for all of my sins. I know that I am a sinner and I cannot get to heaven through good deeds. However, I believe that Jesus died on the cross for my sins, was buried, and that He rose again. I turn from my sins and believe that Jesus alone can save me. I want to be a follower of Jesus and His Word. Come into my life and save my soul. In Jesus' name, Amen."

After Salvation

Wherefore he is able also to save them to the uttermost that come unto God by him, seeing he ever liveth to make intercession for them.

~ **Hebrews 7:25**

The power and promise of God to save and deliver man is so strong that if man has truly experienced His grace and mercy, he would not stray from the course of salvation. However, many have erred due to not fully understanding the obligation that a recipient of salvation has in this mighty act that God has performed on mankind. The following areas detail vital practices that should be practiced regularly by those that are saved:

1. *Win others to Christ* (Pro. 11:30; 1 Cor. 9:22; James 5:20)
2. *Keep a practice of repentance for sin* (1 Tim. 4:16)

The Apostle Paul in in 1 Timothy 4:16, instructs Timothy to pay attention to his actions and conduct and to the teaching of the Word. Paul's purpose is to encourage him in these practices so that he will continue to be diligent in working out his salvation in fear and trembling. Man is to work out or exercise his salvation. God has already given us salvation by grace (His undeserved gift), but to get into the strength of all God has done, he must apply the Word, seek after God's heart, stay pure from the contaminants of the world and build a strong relationship with the LORD (Philippians 2:12).

Find a Suitable Church and Serve

Becoming a member of a suitable church and serving keeps you accountable. No one should be a lone ranger when it comes to Christianity. Oftentimes individuals are dealing with some of the same pressures or issues. It is therefore essential that a Christian Brother or Sister be utilized as a support for struggles one is experiencing (Acts 2:47; 1 Cor. 1:21; Heb. 10:25; 13:17).

Stay in the Word of God

Paul states it best. Scripture is given for doctrine or teaching, to convict about wrongdoing, to correct what is wrong and to instruct one on how to be righteous (2 Tim. 3:16). In reading the Word of God for understanding man learns God's heart and therefore gains the knowledge of the truth needed to walk in the truth received (Luke 8:12; Rom. 1:16; 1 Tim. 2:3-4; 2 Tim. 3:16; 2 Pet. 1:20-21; James 1:21).

This is the same process that you are commissioned to take others through who need salvation. Don't be afraid to go under bridges, embrace the homeless, and witness the Gospel of Jesus Christ to the drug dealers and prostitutes. From the small to the great, and from the rich to the poor, meet them where they are, just as He met you where you were.

CHAPTER 4

"A TRIP DOWN THE ROMANS ROAD"

The Romans Road is an evangelistic process to help lead non-Christians to salvation by using verses from the Roman epistle. This procedure utilizes four key verses from the Book of Romans, which include Romans 3:23, 5:8, 6:23, and 10:9. As we go on this journey through Romans, we will briefly discuss God's judgment of sin, humanity's need for salvation, how salvation was provided, how one can receive salvation, and the results of salvation through Jesus Christ.

Who Wrote Romans and Why is This Significant?

Romans was probably written around 55-57 A.D. Romans 1:1 identifies the author of the Book of Romans as the apostle Paul, however, chapter 16 indicates that Paul likely employed an amanuensis named Tertius to transcribe his words. Today, we call them *ghostwriters*. Tertius was likely Paul's scribe, and he inserted his own salutation at the conclusion of Romans (Rom. 16:22). Paul's utilization of such professionals can also be confirmed at the conclusion of 1 Corinthians 16 when Paul wrote, "The salutation of me Paul with mine own hand." In 2 Thessalonians 3, Paul concludes by saying, "The salutation of me Paul with mine own hand, which is the token in every epistle: so I write." This is proof that Paul used a ghostwriter to transcribe his words, but occasionally, he would personally write his own salutation at the conclusion of his authorships.

Who is the Epistle of Romans Written to and Why?

The epistle of Romans was written to the churches in Rome. The principal reason being was to simply articulate the gospel of grace. Paul also sought to address rising tensions between the Jewish and Gentile (non-Jewish) Christians upon the return of the Jewish Christians after the end of their exile under the rule of the Roman emperor Claudius. According to the Roman historian Suetonius: "Emperor Claudius expelled all the Jews from Rome in 49 AD 'because they were constantly rioting at the instigation of Chrestus (probably Christ).' When Christianity was brought to Rome, there were approximately thirteen synagogues in the city; some were open to the teachings of the Christians regarding Jesus Christ (called "Chrestus" by Suetonius), while others fought against those teachings. This tension led to a clash between the synagogues that was so serious that Claudius responded by forcing all the Jews to leave the city. The Jews expelled by Claudius included not only practitioners of Judaism, but also Jewish Christians. St. Luke tells us that Ss. Aquila and Priscilla went to Corinth (where they met St. Paul) because they were among the Jews expelled by Claudius (Acts 18:2). The Jews were allowed to return to Rome five years later, at the beginning of Emperor Nero's reign in 54 AD."[14] The immorality and growing animosity between

Jewish and Gentile Christians became so intense that it led many to worship separately in houses instead of together in the synagogues (Rom. 16:5). Paul challenged the entire assembly of Roman Christians to show grace to fellow believers who, for reasons of personal conviction, followed different rules regarding dietary standards, and other religious practices.

How does God view Our Sin according to Romans?

God is repulsed by our sins. First, because it is the complete opposite of His nature (Isa. 59:2-4). Second, sin causes us to alienate ourselves from God (Gen. 3:4-11). It is imperative to recognize that in Romans 7, Paul explains that, in our union with Jesus, we died to the law, and subsequently died to sin. The law can no longer act against us because our former man dies in Christ. However, this does not relinquish us from our responsibility to obedience to God's Holy standards. Paul said, "What shall we say then? Shall we continue in sin, that grace may abound? God forbid. How shall we that are dead to sin live any longer therein? (Rom. 6:1-2)" This newness of life in Jesus Christ means that our old sin nature is retroactively crucified, no longer allowing us to be slaves to sin, but able to overcome sin through Jesus Christ.

What is the significance of Adam and Eve covering themselves in Genesis 3?

When Adam and Eve sinned, the Bible says their eyes were opened and as a result of their nakedness, they sewed fig leaves together and tried to hide from God. No longer was their scope of thinking innocent. The effects of sin cause them to perceive themselves in a way God did not purpose. In fact, their nakedness was not an issue—it was their sin and fallen perception of themselves in relation to God's standards. Also, they sought to rely on their own abilities, to provide and secure themselves, rather than rely on God as they had always done.

How did God cover Adam and Eve in Genesis 3?

The Bible says, "And the LORD God said, Behold, the man is become as one of us, to know good and evil: and now, lest he put forth his hand, and take also of the tree of life, and eat, and live forever: Therefore the LORD God sent him forth from the garden of Eden, to till the ground from whence he was taken. So he drove out the man; and he placed at the east of the garden of Eden Cherubims, and a flaming sword which turned every way, to keep the way of the tree of life" (Gen. 3:22-24). The purpose for God's exile of Adam and Eve from the Garden was to keep them from eating from the tree of life, which would have allowed them to live forever. If Adam and Eve had eaten from the tree of life, they would have lived in a perpetual state of sin, along with the future generations of humanity. Sin would have had a permanent hold on all of humanity. God's decision to exile them from the Garden was an act of grace, not punishment. God's ultimate plan was to redeem humanity through the atoning sacrifice of his Son, Jesus Christ, and restore humanity to a state of righteousness and moral purity (Rev. 21:4).

What can be used to address individuals that say they are already morally Good?

The Bible is very clear concerning how "all have sinned, and come short of the glory of God" (Rom. 3:23). Therefore, regardless of how morally good we consider ourselves to be, we still fall short of the standard that God has for us. Paul later says, "For I know that in me (that is, in my flesh,) dwelleth no good thing: for to will is present with me; but how to perform that which is good I find not" (Rom. 7:18). Isaiah said, we are all unclean, and all of our moral virtues are as filthy rags to God. The Greek transliteration for filthy is עֵד, ed (ayd) or "menstrual flux." God is so holy and pure that even our best deeds, done with pure motives are still like filthy soiled menstrual clothes in his sight (Isa. 64:6). Hence, therein remains our need for the atoning grace of Jesus Christ. John said, "If we say that we have no sin, we deceive ourselves, and the truth is not in us. However, God can be trusted to forgive and cleanse us of all our unrighteousness" (1 John 1:8-9). The only person according to the Biblical text that has never sinned was Jesus Christ (1 Pet. 2:22; 1 John 3:5). Right standing with God is not contingent on how morally good we think we are, but on the redemptive authority of confessing Jesus Christ as Lord and Savior, and living according to His commandments (Rom. 10:9).

How did God commend His Love toward Us?

"But God commendeth his love toward us, in that, while we were yet sinners, Christ died for us" (Rom. 5:8). Here the term commend means "to demonstrate." God loves us so much that He gave His very best to be a living sacrifice, so that we would have one final atoning measure and direct access to His sovereignty. "For God so loved the world that he gave his only begotten son that whosoever believeth in him should not perish, but have everlasting life" (John 3:16).

Why must man confess Christ as LORD?

"Lord" means master or ruler. Jesus is the One who died on the cross as the sacrifice for our sins. As a result, all men can have hope of salvation through Him, but without Him, that hope is nonexistent. Therefore, your confession to Jesus as Lord becomes one of allegiance to His sovereignty. Jesus said, "I am the way, the truth, and the life: no man cometh unto the Father, but by me" (John 14:6). According to John's letter, there is no other way to salvation other than by confessing Jesus Christ as Lord (Rom. 10:9-10).

What is the significance of the resurrection in the life of the believer?

According to 1 Corinthians 15, the resurrection of Jesus Christ validates spiritual resurrection for the believer, undoes the authority of sin over the life of the believer, and represents victory over the law, sin and death. Paul also stated:

"Therefore we are buried with him by baptism into death: that like as Christ was raised up from the dead by the glory of the Father, even so we also should walk in newness of life. For if we have been planted together in the likeness of his death, we shall be also in the likeness of his resurrection: Knowing this, that our old man is crucified with him, that the body of sin might be destroyed, that henceforth we should not serve sin"

~ Romans 6:4-6

According to Paul, Jesus' death indicates the death of sin's dominion over the life of the Christian. Paul goes on to emphasize that the Christian's death with Jesus also serves as the sole component that enables separation from the power of sin. Jesus' resurrection is the evidence that not only is the believer spiritually dead to sin, but the believer is alive through the grace of God. Jesus' resurrection serves as proof that He can also raise us up from any figurative or literal form of death.

Where does man's righteousness come from?

According to the testimony of Paul, there are none that have achieved righteousness based on their own merit (Rom. 3:10). Within Paul's letter, he goes on to say that by one man's (Adam) disobedience, many were made sinners. However, through the obedience of Jesus Christ, many will be made righteous (Rom. 5:19). The transliterated word for righteous within this particular text comes from the Greek word dikaios (dik'-ah-yos) meaning justified. Although we deserve damnation because of sin, the sacrifice of Jesus grants us access to forgiveness by confession and belief in Him (Rom. 6:23, 10:9). As a result, He becomes our defense.

Notes

CHAPTER 5

"ETERNITY: HEAVEN, HELL, AND THE JUDGEMENT"

"Behold, what manner of love the Father hath bestowed upon us, that we should be called the sons of God: therefore the world knoweth us not, because it knew him not. Beloved, now are we the sons of God, and it doth not yet appear what we shall be: but we know that, when he shall appear, we shall be like him; for we shall see him as he is. And every man that hath this hope in him purifieth himself, even as he is pure."

~ 1 John 3:1-3

Death affects 100% of the people alive in the world. Everyone living has his appointment with death, regardless of what pains he may take to avoid such an end. Current statistics put the number of people dying on a daily basis at 250,000 per day. There is hope to this culmination to life on earth. Though death affects all, it is also made known by the scriptures that all have eternal life. Upon the conclusion of this temporal existence begins the ascent into eternity. Mankind is in error thinking that within this life one is not held accountable for his actions. Scripture is very explicit on the topics of eternity, the locations of heaven and hell, and the judgment. All will live forever. Based on the deeds done in the body during the finite life led on earth, man will either go to heaven or hell. This chapter seeks to clarify the significance of the teaching on this subject of eternal destination and give one room to ponder the question of eternity: If you were to die today where would you go, heaven or hell?

Judgment

It is essential that judgment be properly identified in context of scripture. Man is either justified or condemned by his confession of faith or lack thereof. If an individual confesses Christ as Lord and Savior and believes in his heart that God raised Him from the dead (Romans 10:9), scripturally he is saved and justified in God's sight. This action positions the individual to heaven. In contrast, if an individual does not accept Christ as Savior in the model mentioned previously, he is condemned to hell (John 3:18). The basis of this initial positioning is the contents of the book of life (Rev. 3:5; 20:12, 15; 21:27).

Heaven

In America, approximately 85% of this nation believes that it is Christian or when asked makes the statement that they are Christians. Some cite that America is a Christian nation and citizenship is the only prerequisite. Others state that they are affiliated with a certain Christian denomination which grants them claim to all that God has promised in His Word. And further still another segment of this group has a family member in a ministerial position within a church body and feels this entitles them to the gift of salvation provided by the Father. However, Christ states that He is the way, the truth and the life, and that no man can come to the Father except through Him (John 14:6).

Man must recognize the significance to accepting Christ as Lord. God the Father gave His best so that those which He loved could have a way to eternal life (John 3:16). If God gave His best, He expects man to receive of His best. In rejecting His gift, man rejects his only means of redemption back to God since works, affiliation and traditions are unable to accomplish this redemptive work (Eph. 2:8; Heb. 10:4). Furthermore, Christ stipulates that the pure in heart alone possess the ability to see God (Matt. 5.8; Heb. 12:14); a state of being impossible to the unrepentant in heart to achieve (1 Pet. 4:17-19).

Heaven in context of scripture is an intermediate home for the believer as he is to inhabit the New Earth (Rev. 21:1). This heaven, just like the New Earth is a physical, literal place. Christ dwells there and is said to be seated on the right hand of the Father. There are several references in scripture in which heaven is used in comparison with God's creating the earth and seas (Ex. 20:11; Jer. 23:24, 31:37). There are also scriptures detailing physical space being inhabited. The use of Christ in heaven dwelling is significant since it denotes that Christ in His glorified body is able to dwell in this location as He did on earth. Therefore, man should understand that in heaven he has a body as he awaits the judgment as outlined in scripture (Jer. 23:24, 31:37; Luke 10:20).

Hell

The choice of mankind's eternal destination begins and ends with Jesus Christ. No decision is a decision for destruction since it denies the evidence provided for the acceptance of Christ as Lord and Savior. Hell has been depicted by secular society as a party, a place where everyone will congregate without pain or punishment or even purgatory. Universalist and Jehovah's Witnesses claim that there is no hell and man simply will cease to be or enter an intermediate state similar to purgatory to be purged from sin. This is of course completely unscriptural and therefore unsound doctrinally. Hell is defined as a place of torment, a place where the devil, the false prophet and the anti-christ will spend eternity when hell is thrown in the lake of fire, and the destination of those that do not accept Christ for the remission of sins *(2 Pet. 2:4; Matt. 10:28, 23:33; Mark 9:43-44; Luke 12:5)*.

One of the best teachings on what occurs after death is found in the gospels. Jesus expounds upon an unnamed rich man and an individual named Lazarus. The rich man goes to a place of torment while Lazarus is in paradise. The rich man has his full faculties about him, has feelings, expresses compassion for his brothers, and has the same desires and needs he had when living. For someone to state that, "hell is a party, and when you're dead you're done," is completely foolish and discordant to the Holy Scriptures. An individual in hell feels pain, isolation, regret, remorse, and compassion for those still living in sin and the same compulsions experienced while living, such as thirst. However, these longings cannot be filled due to the structure of hell and its state of being for the unbeliever (Luke 16:22-24).

How does one end up in the state of torment? Scripture states that lack of repentance is the reason. God does not desire that any perish and actually rejoices over the repentance of one sinner to righteousness. Believers should not be content with just heaven. Scripture lets mankind know that their works follow and he is judged for what has transpired while on earth (Luke 15:7; Ps. 9:16-17; Pro. 15:11, 24, 27:20; Isa. 5:14; Job 34:22-25, 35:13-14, 36:17; 37:23-24; 1 Thess. 4:16; 2 Thess. 1:7; Heb. 9:24; 1 Pet. 3:22; Rev. 14:13, 21:1-3).

CHAPTER 6

"WHO DO YOU SAY I AM?"

You only need to look at the spectacle of the holiday season and notice the hustle and bustle of men, women, and children with a focus upon shopping lists and gift-giving. We are inundated with the traditions of Christmas that point away from the Christ of Christ-mas. So enthralled is our society on the giving of gifts, that we forget about the greatest gift given of God some 2000 years ago in the city of Bethelehem. Many are offended at the name above all names. They take offense at the name which brings redemption from sin, healing, miracles, and salvation to a world submerged in the vices of their own making. We must understand that though we would seek to move the necessity of Jesus Christ from our lives our constant need for him is readily seen in our very existence. In order to grasp the essence of Jesus Christ, we must first know who He is to us as people.

In the book of Revelation, one of the seven churches

mentioned in chapters two and three is the church at Laodicea. Laodicea is described as a church that is rich, but yet is poor (Revelation 3:17). The church at Laodicea was a rich, trade city controlled by the Roman government on the Lychus River. Colosse was once such a city, but declined over time due to its location and significance in the trading practices of the day. It is interesting to note that the Apostle Paul never personally traveled to Colosse. Partly because of the fact that the epistle to the Colossians is part of the prison epistles, thought to be written by Paul when in prison at Rome. Paul's interest in the Colossian church comes from a minister or possibly the pastor of the Colossians, Epaphras. Apparently, Epaphras was one of the individuals that traveled for Paul bringing him news from other churches. Paul was made aware through Epaphras of the love of the Colossian church (Colossian 1:7-8). However, it is clearly evident that the purpose of Paul's writing is to address false teaching that has found its way into the church. Colossians chapter one is the division of Paul's epistle to the church at Colosse that addresses the person and deity of Jesus Christ (Col. 1:13-14).

Paul initially addresses the purpose of Jesus in His redemptive work on the cross, deliverance (rescue) from the power (jurisdiction) of darkness, and translation into His kingdom. We also note that we have redemption or forgiveness of sins through the blood of Christ. Verse fifteen is an extension of these two verses which begins by stating that Jesus Christ is the image (likeness or representation) of the invisible God. Therefore, it is understood that the purpose of Christ's coming is to make God known. It is further understood that He is one and the same with God the Father since it is noted that He is a partaker and the impetus behind creation.

Jesus was and is the active reason or principle behind creation. Colosse was plagued by the worship of things created, namely angels.

Any reasonable individual should see the limitations in worshipping a created thing. The thing created is always at the mercy of that which created it. As it relates to Christ, we are at His mercy. For not only did He create the things we see within the earth and heavens, but it is by Him that they consist. Consist in this context means, a holding together. Hebrews 1:3 extends this revelation by stating, He upholds all things by the word of His power. Those that mock Christ unknowingly come against the very reason and power of their existence!

The Responses of Matthew (16:13-15)

Within every generation man will be bombarded with the question posed by Jesus to His disciples, "Whom do men say that I the Son of Man am" (Matt. 16:13). Even though the twelve had firsthand information of the humanity and deity of Jesus Christ, they were still subject to the influences of their generation. In modern society man is still plagued with the false perceptions imposed by society's way of thinking. Therefore, it is essential that a clear, scriptural understanding of who Jesus is be established to provide clarity and erase any erroneous understandings of who Jesus Christ was, is, and is yet to be in the lives of mankind at large.

Christ in the Old Testament

Throughout the pages of God's Word one finds images and types of Christ. Melchizedek is one such type of Christ found within Genesis (Gen. 14:18; Ps. 110:4). Another extra-biblical text entitled the Book of Jasher claims Melchizedek to be Noah's son Shem, however, such information is false due to the epistle to the Hebrews explaining Melchizedek's unknown origin (Hebrews 7:3). Herein one sees the impact of Christ's statement of, "before Abraham was I am" (John 8:58).

Jacob (Genesis 32:24-30)

Many while interpreting this excerpt state that Jacob wrestled with himself, but it is clearly evident that there was another entity present in which he struggles against. The "man" mentioned has the ability to bless Jacob, change his name and does not disclose His own name (a point that will be highlighted later). This is evidently a preincarnate manifestation of Christ. Another indicator that this is Christ is the use of *elohim* indicating Christ in His part within the Godhead.

"And the angel of the LORD appeared unto him in a flame of fire out of the midst of a bush: and he looked, and, behold, the bush burned with fire, and the bush was not consumed. 4.And when the LORD saw that he turned aside to see, God called unto him out of the midst of the bush, and said, Moses, Moses. And he said, Here am I."

~ Exodus 3:2, 4

The Exodus passage is very interesting and worth looking further into. At first glance a messenger, an angel is within the bush. Further inspection of the original language within Exodus 3:2, 4 shows that the Angel of the Lord is identified as the LORD (Jehovah) and also God (Elohim) indicating Christ.

Moses

Deuteronomy speaks of a prophet God will raise up from amongst the children of Israel like Moses (Deut. 18:15, 18-19). Subsequent scripture within this text discloses the standards to follow concerning prophecy. This correlation ties in with the person of Christ as detailed in Revelation 19:10, which discloses that the "testimony (evidence given) of Jesus is the spirit of prophecy."

Joshua

Throughout scripture, angels and men are not to be worshipped based on the Decalogue's (Ten Commandments) prohibition of such a practice. Joshua stands before the captain of the host of the LORD (LORD of hosts) and bows down without punishment and worships (Joshua 5:14-15). It is often seen in scripture that worship is shunned from mankind and messengers (angels) will immediately correct misguided worship. In this case, the angel does not correct Joshua and gives additional commands to follow. Again another indication of the deity of the captain of the Lord's host (Judges 6:21-24).

Gideon

Gideon has an encounter with the "Angel of the LORD" in this often misconstrued scripture. Upon understanding being received by Gideon, he proclaims that he has seen the angel of the LORD and God must reassure him that he will not die. Others in scripture had seen angels without fear of death, however, why was it necessary that God reassure Gideon that he would not die? Simply, it was an encounter with God Himself. According to John 1:18, no one has seen God at any time, but Jesus has declared or revealed Him.

Isaiah

The prophecies of Isaiah give a clear and in-depth picture of Christ upon his entry and function within the earth. He would be born of a virgin, He would be God with us, He would be a son by birth and adoption, He would walk in the same authority as God upon earth and when the scholars, well-read theologians and spiritual leaders looked upon Him within His generation, they would not recognize Him as God due to physical appearance and His position in society *(Isaiah 7:14, 9:6, 53:2-5)*. Isaiah alone is a strong proof text for the actuality of Christ in His function as God the Son.

This is What Christ Said About Himself

"That all men should honor the Son, even as they honor the Father. He that honoreth not the Son honoreth not the Father which hath sent him. Verily, verily, I say unto you, He that heareth my word, and believeth on him that sent me, hath everlasting life, and shall not come into condemnation; but is passed from death unto life. Verily, verily, I say unto you, The hour is coming, and now is, when the dead shall hear the voice of the Son of God: and they that hear shall live. For as the Father hath life in himself; so hath he given to the Son to have life in himself; And hath given him authority to execute judgment also, because he is the Son of man" (John 5:23-27). *"Search the Scriptures; for in them ye think ye have eternal life: and they are they which testify of me"* (John 5:39).

As the Word of God is studied and searched, one must keep in mind the sole purpose for the Scriptures describing Jesus Christ. Every jot and tittle comes back to His place in the realm of time as Savior of men. In denying this awesome place of majesty, man denies His only source of hope from the law of sin and death. Eternal life is only through Him, since the pronouncement of the right to the tree of life lies in the words of His mouth over the sum total of a man's life. He is by His admission the authority to execute judgment either to life eternal or death everlasting.

The book of John has the *"I am"* statements that reveal so much about who Christ is to mankind. He is the bread of life; the sustenance of man's day to activity, the driving force of life. He is the light of the world; for without Him all are in darkness in spite of how much of the world's wisdom one acquires. He is the "I AM." He defines the timelessness of God and the all-sufficient, omnipotent power of the same. He is the door of the sheep or the true entryway into the ways and purposes of God. The strength and heart of God is wrapped in Him alone and accessed through Him alone. He is the good shepherd; He is fully entrusted with the care and well-being of His designated fold. The sheep hear him and follow, the sheep are a reflection of His care for them and His sheep are ever-flourishing in His care. He is the resurrection and the life; He is the very power that authorizes and enables the dead in Christ to rise to eternal life with Him. He is the only way to the Father, the only truth untainted by time, circumstance and false intentions, and the impetus for temporal and eternal life. And finally, as the true vine, God the Father has groomed Him to bear fruit of righteousness unto salvation. The life of the plant is Him, the root of the plant is Him and mankind is welcomed to be offshoots of His glory and majesty and drink from the life-giving sap which is Jesus Christ.

Historical Icons That Affirmed Jesus Christ

The following are quotes taken from various historical figures that disclose their belief in Christ and awe at the power He wielded while living as a lowly carpenter and itinerant evangelist. Though His condescension would be beneath most men today, the quotes reveal that He had within His person the power to humble the greatest of leaders, thinkers and laypeople with the sacrifice of His very self for the sins of man.

66 *I know men and I tell you that Jesus Christ is no mere man. Between Him and every other person in the world there is no possible term of comparison. Alexander, Caesar, Charlemagne, and I have founded empires. But on what did we rest the creation of our genius? Upon force. Jesus Christ founded His empire upon love; and at this hour millions of men would die for Him."*

" *Alexander, Caesar, Charlemagne, and I have founded empires. But on what did we rest the creations of our genius? Upon force. Jesus Christ founded his empire upon love; and at this hour millions of men would die for him."* ~ **Napoleon Bonaparte**

" *A man who was completely innocent, offered himself as a sacrifice for the good of others, including his enemies, and became the ransom of the world. It was a perfect act."*

" *I like your Christ, I do not like your Christians. Your Christians are so unlike your Christ."* ~ **Mahatma Gandhi**

" *I am an historian, I am not a believer, but I must confess as a historian that this penniless preacher from Nazareth is irrevocably the very center of history. Jesus Christ is easily the most dominant figure in all history."* ~ **H.G. Wells**

" *As the centuries pass, the evidence is accumulating that, measured by His effect on history, Jesus is the most influential life ever lived on this planet."* ~ **Historian Kenneth Scott Latourette**

" *Fundamentally, our Lord's message was Himself. He did not come merely to preach a Gospel; He himself is that Gospel. He did not come merely to give bread; He said, "I am the bread." He did not come merely to shed light; He said, "I am the light." He did not come merely to show the door; He said, "I am the door." He did not come merely to name a shepherd; He said, "I am the shepherd." He did not come merely to point the way; He said, "I am the way, the truth, and the life."* ~ **J. Sidlow Baxter**

Who Do You Say I AM?

" *Jesus is the God whom we can approach without pride and before whom we can humble ourselves without despair."* ~ **Blaise Pascal**

" *As a child I received instruction both in the Bible and in the Talmud. I am a Jew, but I am enthralled by the luminous figure of the Nazarene....No one can read the Gospels without feeling the actual presence of Jesus. His personality pulsates in every word. No myth is filled with such life."* ~ **Albert Einstein**

" *There is something so pure and frank and noble about Him that to doubt His sincerity would be like doubting the brightness of the sun."*
~ **Charles Edward Jefferson**

" *A man who was merely a man and said the sort of things Jesus said would not be a great moral teacher. He would either be a lunatic – on a level with the man who says he is a poached egg – or else he would be the Devil of Hell. You must make your choice. Either this man was, and is, the Son of God; or else a madman or something worse. You can shut Him up for a fool, you can spit at Him and kill him as a demon; or you can fall at His feet and call Him Lord and God. But let us not come with any patronizing nonsense about His being a great human teacher. He has not left that open to us. He did not intend to."* ~ **C.S. Lewis**

" *Jesus Christ is to me the outstanding personality of all time, all history, both as Son of God and as Son of Man. Everything he ever said or did has value for us today and that is something you can say of no other man, dead or alive. There is no easy middle ground to stroll upon. You either accept Jesus or reject him."* ~ **Sholem Asch**

" *Jesus is God spelling Himself out in language that men can understand."*
~ **S.D. Gordon**

❝ *I accept the resurrection of Easter Sunday not as an invention of the community of disciples, but as a historical event. If the resurrection of Jesus from the dead on that Easter Sunday were a public event which had been made known...not only to the 530 Jewish witnesses but to the entire population, all Jews would have become followers of Jesus."* ~ **Pinchas Lapide, Orthodox Jewish scholar, Germany (born 1922)**

❝ *I would like to ask Him if He was indeed virgin born, because the answer to that question would define history."* ~ **Larry King**

❝ *The Lord ate from a common bowl, and asked the disciples to sit on the grass. He washed their feet, with a towel wrapped around His waist - He, who is the Lord of the universe!"* ~ **Clement of Alexandria**

Throughout this chapter several scriptures have been given as proof-texts of the deity of Christ. But, one must still answer for oneself, "Who do you say He is?" God the Father has given mankind no other way to rectify the dirt and filth of sin. Jesus is the only way to the provisions of the Father's love. His wrath is poured out on sin. The law decrees the punishment for anyone caught within its clutches. Whether a liar, a fornicator, a thief, it doesn't matter which sin one is guilty of, sin is sin and God will punish the individual that fails to escape through the only means given by God to do so, the blood of Jesus Christ. Unlike times past when man atoned for sin through the blood of animals, God gave His only begotten Son, that whosoever believes in Him shall not perish, but shall have everlasting life. Therefore, to this end, only believe.

CHAPTER 7

"COMMON EXCUSES"

"For the invisible things of him from the creation of the world are clearly seen, being understood by the things that are made, even his eternal power and Godhead; so that they are without excuse."

~ Romans 1:20

Excuses, whether good or bad are prevalent in current society. Therefore, it is of no surprise that individuals would hide behind excuses to bypass God's grace and be saved. It is so much easier to blame my shortcomings on the economy, my upbringing, my friends, and even the weather. But ultimately, all must give an account to God for things they have done or left undone. The current chapter focuses on excuses and invites the reader to view excuses from this point in light of eternity. Will something as petty as the excuses discussed be a means to keep someone from entrance to God's kingdom? Scripture gives plain indication of this reality. Therefore, the Christian Apologist must insure that he is effective at disclosing the Good News of Jesus Christ's atoning work for mankind.

I have plenty of time/I'm not ready,,,

These excuses are rather similar and will be grouped and addressed accordingly. First, the scenario is this, an individual has heard the gospel, there is an acknowledgement of sin, knowledge of Christ and His sacrifice, and the details of what the individual must do to receive the gift of salvation from God. However, instead of being the recipient of God's grace the individual states that either they have plenty of time or are just not ready. Does one respect this viewpoint or push further? Salvation should never be forced, remember it is a free gift that is undeserved, however, the individual should be made aware of what the Word of God says about our time and readiness to receive God's gift of salvation.

"The night is far spent, the day is at hand: let us therefore cast off the works of darkness, and let us put on the armor of light. Let us walk honestly, as in the day; not in rioting and drunkenness, not in chambering and wantonness, not in strife and envying."

~ Romans 13:12-13

The verses prior to Psalm 90:12 discuss God's wrath and His view on man's conduct. God is wrathful toward disobedience. It is sin that separates man from God, sin puts mankind in a state of hostility toward God and institutes God's wrath upon mankind. The Psalmist states that man should apply his heart unto wisdom through the practice of numbering or accounting for his days. Day also signifies heat or time when the world is lit by the sun. When an individual preaches the gospel of Christ to a sinner, there is enlightenment and with that light comes the responsibility to walk in the new revelation received.

"For he saith, I have heard thee in a time accepted, and in the day of salvation have I succored thee: behold, now is the accepted time; behold, now is the day of salvation."

~ 2 Corinthians 6:2

There is no reason to wait on salvation. Today is the day. If an individual states that they agree with what has been presented, yet still don't want to accept Christ, it is nothing against the Christian Apologist personally, it is a rejection of Christ as Savior and Lord. Remind individuals which are receiving ministry of their obligation to respond to the Word of God in love. In all ministry to the lost, look at them with the anticipation and longing that God showed in His coming in sinful flesh to redeem mankind.

I am a good Person...

"Making the word of God of none effect through your tradition, which ye have delivered: and many such like things do ye."

~ Mark 7:13

"For I say unto you, That except your righteousness shall exceed the righteousness of the scribes and Pharisees, ye shall in no case enter into the kingdom of heaven."

~ Matthew 5:20

Americans have been lied to and told that they are automatically declared a Christian just from affiliation with the United States through birth or naturalization. However, man has the problem of sin that must be addressed. Contrary to popular belief, works will not get one into glory, neither will affiliations, or self-imposed discipline or asceticism. Therefore, it's not enough to simply attend church, be affiliated to a particular denomination, or be an American. Man must go through Jesus Christ. If one has not declared Jesus Christ as Lord and repented, he cannot enter the kingdom of heaven as scripture describes. Salvation should be viewed as being 'saved' from drowning. When overcome with the winds and water and feeling oneself going under, one feels the helplessness, the uncertainty and the longing of someone to bring them to safety.

The Bible has too many errors in it. How can I know the Bible is true, and how can I trust that the Jesus presented in the Bible is the truth?

God has made promises to mankind concerning His Word. Scripture describes the Word as pure (Ps. 30:5), given by inspiration of God, profitable for teaching, bringing conviction and not of private interpretation (2 Tim. 3:16). The fact that the scripture is not of private interpretation or as indicated by the original language a separate application or script, is of vital importance to understanding the truth found in the Bible. Regardless of what has occurred throughout history, the Bible as God's Word to man has remained in the form He intended for him to receive it. Several prophecies relate the man Jesus Christ as the promised Messiah of the scripture, archaeological evidence supports the authenticity of the Bible and the Old and New Testaments are authenticated by history itself. In addressing these excuses, one must ask how someone knows the newspaper they receive each day is true, the magazine discussing their favorite artist, actor, musician or other prominent figure is true or even when someone discloses their name and life details. How does truth become established in the mind? If someone can accept a newspaper or magazine to be truthful, it is highly likely that such an individual can accept God's Word is true as well.

I have some habits I don't want to give up...

"For what is a man profited, if he shall gain the whole world, and lose his own soul? or what shall a man give in exchange for his soul?"

~ **Matthew 16:26**

A habit is defined in the 1828 Webster's Dictionary of the American Language as a state of being and in older context a type of clothing that individuals put on. If someone states that they have things that they are unwilling to part with it is indication of a lack of understanding of God's wrath. If an individual is unwilling to yield to God to spend another day or series of days in the "attire of sin" they are basically exchanging the value of their soul, which is priceless, for the pleasures of the world. In making provision for the flesh, an individual seeks out the temporary without knowing the extent of their lives or the implications of current actions on eternity. Remind the individual in love of the implications of their decision and what God says about the temporary status of the terrestrial earth.

"Study to show thyself approved unto God, a workman that needeth not to be ashamed, rightly dividing the word of truth."

~ **2 Timothy 2:15**

The Christian Apologist must address each excuse with the light of scripture. This means a Christian Apologist must be a student of the Word of God. There isn't always room for extensive study in all the particulars of life. But, immersing one's self in the Scriptures and seeking its light and pulling from the essence of God's nature. This is essential to address the myriad of excuses that individuals are certain to bring in response to the gospel's truth.

SECTION I

"ENGAGING OTHER BELIEFS"

AGNOSTICISM

"GOD'S EXISTENCE IS UNKNOWN"

Agnostics believe that existence of a deity is unknown or unknowable. Since God cannot be known in the human estimation according to the agnostic, Christ cannot be served and received as Savior. The miracles performed by Christ in the agnostic's understanding are no more than exaggerations of the Biblical authors and where miracles are proved, if proven, they are no more than aberrant scientific anomalies that should be examined further in light of new scientific discoveries and understanding.

HISTORICAL BACKGROUND

Agnostic was a term coined by Thomas Huxley in his book the *Ethics of Belief*. The word itself is derived from the Greek equivalent of without (*a-*) and knowledge (*-gnosis*). Since the agnostic belief, based on Huxley's estimation, states that belief must have a demonstration within the realm of the physical senses. Where God cannot make Himself known to the physical senses, He is an entity that cannot be known and therefore unworthy of worship by the agnostic.

The agnostic must understand that although something does not exist in the realm of the senses, it is not a clear indicator that it cannot be known. Scientists have long made discoveries of things that seemingly did not exist in the realm of the senses. Even in one's own physical body, individuals are led to know that there are internal systems that dictate external realities. If someone has a headache, though someone cannot see it, taste it, hear it or feel it, it does not nullify the fact that the particular headache exists and that it can occur in the life, better the body of another individual. Further, if forty unrelated individuals tell someone about the reality of a headache, is it not worth examination?

"For the invisible things of him from the creation of the world are clearly seen, being understood by the things that are made, even his eternal power and Godhead; so that they are without excuse:"

~ Romans 1:20

"For what if some did not believe? shall their unbelief make the faith of God without effect? God forbid: yea, let God be true, but every man a liar; as it is written, That thou mightest be justified in thy sayings, and mightest overcome when thou art judged."

~ Romans 3:3-4

WITNESSING TO THE AGNOSTIC

We have found the Way of the Master method to be quite effective when witnessing to the Agnostic. Visit www.wayofthemaster.com

Notes

ATHEISM

"THERE IS NO GOD"

"Atheist seem to need concrete evidence that God exist, but don't seem to need concrete evidence that He does not exist. Give that some thought."

~ Kenny Fry

Atheism is one of those belief systems that are a kind of non-religion. Almost all definitions and subsequent practices pertaining to religion are geared toward adherence to some type of supernatural power or deity. In the case of atheism, there is no supernatural power. Atheist believe that there are no deities to speak of as is the practice of many other belief systems. An atheist is a person who denies or disbelieves the existence of a Supreme Being or creator.

HISTORICAL BACKGROUND

The expression atheist originates from the Greek word Atheos *(ath'-eh-os)* meaning godless or without God (Eph. 2:12). The term atheist is a combination of two Greek words *A (al'-fah)*, the first letter in the English and Greek alphabet, and theos *(theh'-os)* meaning a deity; supreme divinity; God.

An atheist relies heavily on philosophical reasoning, scientific method, humanism and secular skepticism toward the existence of God or any deity for that matter. Atheist believe that religion, especially Christianity is of human origin and cannot withstand the scrutiny of scientific inquiring, philosophical debate and logical reasoning.

The atheist would believe that the person of Jesus Christ in the Christian belief is a human concoction to control the mentally inferior. As a personal note to the Christian apologist, many writers of the scriptures were learned men and able to dialogue in the philosophies of the day, for example, Moses trained in all the arts, sciences, and cultural practices of the Egyptians; Daniel, the prophet, was adept at science; Isaiah, the prophet, was likened to a diplomat or statesman; Luke, the physician, and the Apostle Paul argued Christ before some of the renown philosophical practitioners of their day on Mars Hill in Athens. Therefore, it is readily known that if Christianity has the ability to sway the minds of men of such educational prowess, it is at least worth looking into.

WITNESSING TO AN ATHEIST

In approaching the atheist, one should expound on the fact that a fair examination of the scriptures should be attempted. Many skeptics of the Holy Writ have been swayed after carefully considering their own prejudices or questions to the authenticity of Scripture and fairly gauging them with purposeful personal study to judge them as true or not. Upon such an examination, the Holy Spirit can have His way in the mind and, ultimately, in the life of the skeptical atheist.

"Come now, and let us reason together, saith the LORD: though your sins be as scarlet, they shall be as white as snow; though they be red like crimson, they shall be as wool." ~ **Isaiah 1:18**

"But God hath chosen the foolish things of the world to confound the wise; and God hath chosen the weak things of the world to confound the things which are mighty; And base things of the world, and things which are despised, hath God chosen, yea, and things which are not, to bring to naught things that are: That no flesh should glory in his presence.
~ **1 Corinthians 1:27-29**

Common mistakes made by Christians when dialoguing with atheists are:

1. Identifying Atheists

Some Christians have labeled atheists as evil, unintelligent, devil-worshippers, or morally void. Though there may be some atheists who fit these categories (as would many in the general population), atheists are not categorically evil, unintelligent, devil-worshipping, or immoral degenerates. Many of them are fine citizens, honest, caring, loving, and patient. For a Christian, or anyone for that matter, to generalize atheists in a derogatory manner is wrong. It is the same thing atheists sometimes do when they accuse Christians of being irrational, psychotic, or stupid. Such accusations have no place on either side of the argument of truth.

Generally speaking, atheists are not unintelligent. Many of them have thought through their position over a long period of time and arrive at conclusions after much thought. Some were raised in religious homes, have seen what religion has to offer, and have rejected it. Of course, we believe that atheists have drawn incorrect conclusions about God, but it doesn't mean they are dumb. Some atheists have presented very cogent arguments against the existence of God, which need to be addressed.

So, just because someone believes in God and encounters someone who doesn't, that does not mean that either side is stupid. Therefore, labeling and name-calling have no place within any discussion.

"But speaking the truth in love, may grow up into him in all things, which is the head, even Christ: From whom the whole body fitly joined together and compacted by that which every joint supplieth, according to the effectual working in the measure of every part, maketh increase of the body unto the edifying of itself in love." ~ **Ephesians 4:15-16**

2. Ignoring Atheists' Questions

If you were standing on a railroad track and a train was heading your way, closing your eyes and ignoring the locomotive will not make it go away. If an atheist asks a question and you ignore it repeatedly, it would be fair for him to conclude you were incapable of answering the objection. Of course, this does not mean you have to always answer everything because dialogue flows both ways. But, it is important that you face hard questions. If you don't have an answer, admit it. That's okay. It doesn't mean you are wrong. It simply means you don't have an answer. Go study, get an answer, and get back to him or her.

3. Stating that Atheism is a Religion

Atheists will repeatedly tell you that they are not in a religion. A religion almost always is defined to include belief in a deity of some sort. Atheism is non-belief in a deity. It isn't necessarily a "belief that there is no God," (though it can be) but is "not believing either way."

To label an atheist as a religious person is to put up a roadblock to effective communication. It would be like someone saying to a Christian, "You believe in a mean, tyrannical being who likes to torture people." The Christian would simply roll his eyes and think that the person doesn't know what he's talking about. So, how much effective conversation could there be in either instance? Not much.

4. Stating Unsupportable Facts

No one has all documentation for everything they say. Therefore, it is not reasonable to require proof from an atheist on everything said. Nevertheless, if you are going to state a fact or two, it is good to have a reference at the tip of your tongue and, at least occasionally, have access to it. It adds to your credibility. Of course, references or documentation isn't necessary for everything, but if you have some illustrious fact to use, try to have it available.

5. Never Admitting when You are Wrong

Pride is a harmful thing. It caused the fall. It ruins marriages. It leads to anger and self-righteousness. Therefore, it has no place in the Christian's life. Not admitting that you are wrong is being prideful. If an atheist, or anyone else, proves you wrong about something, be kind and courteous. Admit you were wrong and go on. Everyone makes mistakes, even atheist.

There is nothing wrong with admitting an error. It no more disproves your knowledge regarding Christianity than being wrong about the time of day. But, if you never admit when you are wrong, you will not be able to convince anyone in a discussion of your position. You will simply lose the respect of the one with whom you are debating.

FUNDAMENTAL ARGUMENTS FOR ATHEISM

In addition, according to Norman L. Geisler and Lanny Wilson, there exist several positive arguments for atheism, and they believe that these arguments fall into four categories: (1) the fact of evil; (2) purposelessness of life; (3) random universal occurrences; and (4) the First Law of Thermodynamics.

1. The Existence of Evil

In his book "A Case for Christianity," C.S. Lewis, a former atheist turned Christian, said, "God created things which had free will. That means creatures which can go wrong or right. Some people think they can imagine a creature which was free but had no possibility of going wrong, but we can't. If a thing is free to be good it's also free to be bad. Free will is what has made evil possible. Why then did God give them free will? Because free will, though it makes evil possible, is also the only thing that makes possible any love, goodness, or joy worth having. A world of automata (creatures that work like machines) would hardly be worth creating. The happiness which God designs for His higher creatures is the happiness of being freely, voluntarily united to Him and to each other in an ecstasy of love and delight compared with which the most rapturous love between a man and a woman on this earth is mere milk and water. And for that they've got to be free."

2. The Purposelessness of Life

Many atheists prematurely ascribe to a false notion that life has no meaning. How can the atheist truly know that existence has no significance or purpose? The Christian apologist should ask the atheist for evidence of such claims, and follow up with verses that oppose such a view. (See Genesis 1:1; Jeremiah 29:11; Proverbs 16:4; John 1:1 -3; Hebrews 1:10)

3. Random Occurrences in the Universe

Random occurrences neither prove nor disprove the existence of God. First, let's properly define the term "random." The most fundamental Western use of the term random or randomness is defined as, *a haphazard course; lacking a definite plan, purpose, or pattern.* Some atheists may say that the existence of patterns does not contradict the existence of randomness. The truth of the matter is, regardless of how the atheist tries to obscure or redefine the term, it does in fact contradict the true definition of randomness. Consider a woman that utilizes a pregnancy test, which indicates to her that she is pregnant. She goes to the doctor, who does blood work and later tells her that she is not pregnant, but that the test exhibited a false-positive result. Truth, the woman is not pregnant. However, does this random occurrence disprove or interrupt that truth? Randomness does neither. Instead, it will prompt the one that is aware of the occurrence toward further investigation in order to come to a reasonable and evidence-based conclusion of the matter. In other words, it will prompt the recipient to seek for truth, whether the results prove to be agreeable or disagreeable. How the recipient responds to truth is up to them. Jesus said, "I am the way, the truth, and the life: no one comes to the father, except through me" (John 14:6).

Furthermore, carefully consider the occurrences that some atheists deem to be random. Whether they will admit it or not, is it possible that those are merely occurrences that the atheist cannot predict? When one faces this possibility, they must also come face to face with the reality that their limited knowledge disables them from coming to any dependable truth claims regarding the viewpoint of random occurrence (1 Cor. 1:27-31; Isa. 29:14, 19; 2 Cor. 4:7).

THE LAWS OF THERMODYNAMICS

1. The First Law of Thermodynamics

In reality, there are four basic laws of thermodynamics (starting from zero to the third). The First Law of Thermodynamics states that energy can neither be created nor destroyed. Dr. Henry Morris called this the "principle of conservation," which theoretically shows that the universe is eternal and, therefore, needs no Creator. Scientifically, these concepts received notable recognition in the 19th century with scientists like Rudolf Clausius, William Rankine, William Thomson, and Emile Clapeyron.

The very terms themselves express contradictory concepts. The word "evolution" is derived from a Latin word meaning "out-rolling". The picture is of an outward-progressing spiral, an unrolling from an infinitesimal beginning through ever broadening circles, until finally all reality is embraced within. "Entropy" on the other hand, means literally "in-turning." It is derived from the two Greek words *en* (meaning "in") and *trope* (meaning "turning"). The concept is of something spiraling inward upon itself, the exact opposite concept to "evolution." Evolution is "change outward and upward, entropy is change inward and downward" (Evolution, Thermodynamics, and Entropy, by Henry Morris, Ph.D., icr.org).

Atheists that use the argument of thermodynamics erroneously interject that the universe is eternal, and, therefore, needs no Creator. The First Law of Thermodynamics makes no statement about the origin or destruction of energy; nor does it discuss the eternality of energy. But, atheist still hold to their assertions.

2. The Second Law of Thermodynamics

The Second Law of Thermodynamics (also known as The Law of Increased Entropy) crushes the First Law by stating that energy gradually deteriorates over time. In other words, things rot, decay, and rust. Eventually, everything gets old and falls apart. Alternatively, the Second Law confounds those who hold to the First Law.

Nevertheless, if the First Law of Thermodynamics is true, is it possible that it can be defied like the Law of Gravity. Is it possible that there exist some laws that cannot be broken by mere man, but can be altered by an omnipotent Creator? The first verse of the Bible says, "In the beginning God created the heavens and the earth" (Genesis 1:1). Dr. Morris and other theistic scientists have used the laws of thermodynamics to refute evolution and affirm the existence of God. Moreover, if God did not create the heavens and the earth, what did? What started everything? These are relevant questions for the atheist, but we know that, "By faith we understand that the worlds were framed by the word of God, so that the things which are seen were not made of things which are visible" (Hebrews 11:3).

In his book, *God and the Astronomers*, astrophysicist, Dr. Robert Jastrow explains why attempts to prove an eternal Universe failed. "Now three lines of evidence—the motions of the galaxies, the laws of thermodynamics, and the life story of the stars—pointed to one conclusion; all indicated that the Universe had a beginning" (1978, p. 111). If Jastrow is correct, then Dr. Morris was also correct when he stated in his book *Scientific Creationism* that, "The Second Law requires the universe to have had a beginning" (1974, p. 26). Therefore, if their assertions are true, and we believe they are, then the Universe is not eternal and a Creator must have been its cause.

WITNESSING TO THE ATHEIST

We have found the Way of the Master method to be effective when witnessing to Atheist. Visit www.wayofthemaster.com

Notes

CHRISTIANITY

"THE GOSPEL OF JESUS CHRIST"

According to the Pew Research Center, "A comprehensive demographic study of more than 200 countries found that there are over 2.18 billion Christians in the world, representing nearly a third of the estimated 2010 global population of 6.9 billion."[15] Based on the Pew Research Center, Christianity is currently the world's largest religion in the world.

The followers of Jesus were first called Christians in Antioch (Acts 11:26). Christians are currently the most persecuted religious group worldwide and possibly have been since their inception, even more than Jews. Vatican spokesman Archbishop Silvano Maria Tomasi announced in a radio address to the United Nations Human Rights Council that, "Credible research has reached the shocking conclusion that every year an estimate of more than 100,000 Christians are killed because of some relation to their faith." [16]

Within Northern Africa, the Middle East, China, North Korea, and now the United States of America, Christians continue to experience diverse forms of cruelty from extremist groups, and in many cases from their own governments. Among the 50 worst nations for persecution, Islamic extremists frequently target, pursue, and execute Christians within 41 of those countries. 11 out of the 50 worst nations are experiencing extreme forms of tyranny from unjust imprisonment, torture or murder by drownings, beheadings, or having explosives strapped to their bodies and detonated.[17] John Rhys-Davies said, "Basically, Christianity in the Middle East and in Africa is being wiped out. Not just ideologically but physically, and people are being enslaved and killed because they are Christians."[18]

Currently, North Korea ranks as the #1 worst place to be a Christian. Presently, it is illegal to be a Christian in North Korea and Christians are often sent to labor camps or are killed if they are discovered. The conditions in North Korea have remained the worst in the world for Christians during the past 13 years.[19]

HISTORICAL BACKGROUND

Christianity is a monotheistic religion, meaning that it teaches that there is only one God. Christianity was established upon the teachings and miracles of Jesus, who is also identified as the Christ according to Biblical authorship (see Matt. 1:1, 6; 16:16; Mark 8:29; Luke 2:11; 4:41; 9:20; John 1:41 and 20:31).

Christianity also debunks the concept of evolution by teaching that God is the creator of the Heavens (the universe along with the visible atmosphere around the globe), and the Earth (Gen. 1:1; Heb. 1:10). God created all life that inhabits the Earth. According to the Bible, God created man in His image and in His likeness (Gen. 1:26; 2:7). God created Adam, placed him in the Garden of Eden, and gave the fullness of humanity dominion over all that He had created on the

Earth. God commanded humanity to be fruitful, multiply and replenish the earth, and to subdue or render control over it. Through Adam, God gave all of humanity the autonomy to choose between right and wrong. When God put Adam in the garden, He gave him one commandment: "…of the tree of the knowledge of good and evil, thou shalt not eat of it: for in the day that thou eatest thereof thou shalt surely die" (Gen. 2:16-17). God then created Eve (2:18-25).

Subsequently, Adam and Eve chose to disobey God by eating of the forbidden tree. Due to Adam and Eve's choice to sin (which serves as a reflection of the nature of all their successors), sin entered into world, and brought death upon all mankind (Rom. 5:12; 6:23). According to the Christian faith, sin created within all of humanity an innate egocentric and disobedient disposition (Rom. 7:17-18, 20). Sin brought death and condemnation to all humanity, but according to the Bible, God provided salvation through the atoning sacrifice of His only Begotten (John 3:16). Throughout the books of the prophets (i.e. Isaiah, Jeremiah, Daniel, etc.) the coming of the Savior was foretold:

> "*For unto us a child is born, unto us a son is given: and the government shall be upon his shoulder: and his name shall be called Wonderful, Counsellor, The mighty God, The everlasting Father, The Prince of Peace. [7.]Of the increase of his government and peace there shall be no end, upon the throne of David, and upon his kingdom, to order it, and to establish it with judgment and with justice from henceforth even forever. The zeal of the LORD of hosts will perform this*" (Isaiah 9:6-7).

Also see: Isa. 53:1-12; Jer. 23:5, 33:15-17; Dan. 9:24-26; Zech. 13:7; Luke 18:31-33, 24:46; Matt. 27:53; John 10:18; 1 Cor. 15:3, 20-23.

JESUS CHRIST

The Greek transliteration of Christ is Christos (*khris-tos'*) meaning *anointed one*, that is, the *Messiah*. The term Messiah is an epithet (description) of Jesus, not His last name. However, it remains suitable to identify Him as Jesus Christ (Matt. 1:1, 6, 18; 16:20). According to biblical text, Jesus is the Messiah sent by God the Father to redeem all of humanity, and serves as the fulfillment of Old Testament law and prophecy. His life, death on the cross, and physical resurrection from the dead serve as the evidence of His person and purpose.

John, the revelator, expressed that Jesus performed so many things that are not disclosed in writing, that he supposed that the world could not contain all the books that would be written about Jesus (John 21:25). Christianity teaches that Jesus is the incarnation of God the Father or God in human flesh (John 1:1-14; Rom. 8:3; Eph. 2:15). The most direct statement Jesus made about His deity is found in John 10:30, where He affirms this notion by saying, "I and my Father are one." However, the mystery within the incarnation is that Jesus is fully God and entirely human. According to Paul's words, God humbled Himself by taking on human flesh, placing Himself within a position of servitude to creation, and submitting Himself to death and the Roman method of execution (Phil. 2:5-11).

Furthermore, the Bible is the most unique of all books because it has accurately foretold of thousands of events. The Bible's 100% accuracy rate makes it the most reliable source pertaining to God and His agenda. Moreover, if modern investigators of the Biblical text were to line Bible prophecies with current world events, they would clearly see the fulfillment of the vast majority of Bible prophecies. Christianity teaches *eschatology*, which is the study of "last things." In Christian theology, the term eschatology focuses on the fulfillment of Biblical prophecy, primarily events that are yet to be fulfilled. The Bible teaches that the Lord will come as a thief in the night and carry His followers away to where He is before the occurrence of the Great Tribulation. According to Matthew 24, the Disciples asked Jesus how they would know of his [second] coming. In response, Jesus itemized a list of prophetic occurrences for the Disciples. For the sake of simplicity, we have condensed these prophecies into brief phases:

1. **The Beginning of Sorrows** (Matt. 24:4-8)
    a. Many will come professing to be the Christ (and will deceive many).
    b. There will be wars and rumors of wars
    c. Nation will rise against nation
    d. Kingdom will rise against kingdom
    e. There will be famine
    f. There will be pestilences
    g. Earth quakes in various places

2. **Perilous Times** (Matt. 24:9-14, see also 2 Tim. 3:1)
    a. Christians and Jews will be brought forth to be persecuted, killed
    b. Christians and Jews will be hated by all for His (Jesus) name's sake.
    c. Then will many be offended, betraying and hating one another.
    d. Many false prophets will rise and deceive many.
    e. Since iniquity will increase, the love of many will wax cold
    f. The Gospel of Jesus Christ will be preached to all the world

It is believed that each of these prophecies above were fulfilled by the time Jerusalem fell in A.D. 70.

3. The Rapture (see Matt. 24:36-44; 1 Thess. 4:13-18)

> *"But as the days of Noe were, so shall also the coming of the Son of man be. 38. For as in the days that were before the flood they were eating and drinking, marrying and giving in marriage, until the day that Noe entered into the ark, 39. And knew not until the flood came, and took them all away; so shall also the coming of the Son of man be. 40. Then shall two be in the field; the one shall be taken, and the other left. 41. Two women shall be grinding at the mill; the one shall be taken, and the other left. 42. Watch therefore: for ye know not what hour your Lord doth come."*

> ~ Matthew 24:37-42

Those whose names are written in the Lamb's book of life (Revelation 13:8; 20:12, 15) will be taken out of the world to be with Christ. Paul said, "Then we which are alive *and* remain shall be caught up together with them in the clouds, to meet the Lord in the air: and so shall we ever be with the Lord (1 Thess. 4:17). The term often used to detail this event is *rapture*. The English word "rapture" derives from the Latin verb "rapiemur or rapio" meaning to seize, carry off, or to catch up. The English word rapture is synonymous with the Greek transliteration for harpazo (*har-pad'-zo*) meaning to *seize* (in various applications): - catch (away, up), pluck, pull, or take (by force).

The term rapture means the carrying away of a person to another place or sphere of existence (1 Thess. 4:17). Therefore, while the exact word rapture is not in the Bible, the contextual meaning is there. The rapture is not a predictable period or event, but an instantaneous moment (1 Cor. 15:52; 25:13). Not even the angels in heaven know the moment of the rapture (Mark 13:32).

It is important to note that we believe the rapture is a *pre-tribulation* event. The reason we reject *mid-tribulation* and *post-tribulation* is because they both deny the *doctrine of imminence* (Matt. 25:13). Also, the Church is expressly exempt from experiencing God's wrath (1 Thess. 5:9; Rev. 3:10).

4. **Tribulation Period: 70th week of Daniel** (Dan. 12; Jer. 30:7)
    A. Tribulation (first 3 ½ years of deceitful peace)
        i. The Antichrist will rise into political power becoming the world's chief leader. (Matt. 24:21-28; 1 John 2, 4:3; 2 John 1:7).
        ii. The Antichrist will be embraced by the entire world, which is symbolic of the beast ascending out of the sea (Rev. 13:1-18, 17).
        iii. The Antichrist will form a seven year peace treaty with Israel (Dan. 9:27a)
        iv. The Antichrist will subdue the entire world and form one world government (Dan. 2:40; Rev. 13).
    B. Great Tribulation (second 3 ½ years of war)
        i. The Antichrist will break his treaty with Israel (Dan. 9:27b; 2 Thess. 2:3-4).
        ii. In conjunction with the Antichrist, a false prophet/religious leader will emerge to assist him to form one world theocracy (Rev. 13:11-17).
        iii. The wrath of God is poured out over the earth upon those that worship the beast and accepted his mark (Rev. 14-16).

5. **The [Second] Coming** (Matt. 24:29-31)
        a. The Lord will return and defeat the super powers of the earth, and conquer the rulers of the earth (Rev. 19)
        b. The Lord will return to establish His kingdom and millennial reign (Rev. 20-21).

HISTORICAL NON-CHRISTIAN PROOF FOR JESUS

Beginning with what historian Edwin Yamauchi said was "probably the most important reference to Jesus outside the New Testament."[20] Regarding Emperor Nero's decision to blame Christians for the fire that destroyed Rome in 64 A.D., the Roman historian Publius (or Gaius) Cornelius Tacitus wrote:

> *"Nero fastened the guilt...on a class hated for their abominations, called Christians by the populace. Christus, from whom the name had its origin, suffered the extreme penalty during the reign of Tiberius at the hands of...Pontius Pilatus, and a most mischievous superstition, thus checked for the moment, again broke out not only in Judaea, the first source of the evil, but even in Rome..."*[21]

Notice that Tacitus expresses that the earlier Christians originated their name from a person he identified as Christus (from the Latin), or Christ. It is suspected that Tacitus was born in northern Italy, hence the Latin expression for Christ. Obviously, referring to the Roman form of execution (i.e. crucifixion), Tacitus goes on to mention that Christus "suffered the extreme penalty during the reign of Tiberius at the hands of...Pontius Pilatus." He writes that Christus death occurred during the reign of Tiberius and by the sentence of Pontius Pilatus. Tactitus' writings serve as additional affirmation for the Gospels regarding the death of Jesus.

THE TRINITY

Christianity teaches that God is a Trinity (Father, Son, and Holy Spirit; not three Gods). God, the Father is the first person of the Trinity and He is a Spirit (Gen. 1:1, 26; John 4:24). Jesus Christ is the second person of the Trinity (fully God and fully man), who died on the cross and rose from the dead to redeem all of humanity from the clutches of sin (Rom. 3:23-24, 6:23). The Bible teaches that the acceptance of Jesus is the only way to be saved, and salvation is received by faith in Him alone, not by our own efforts (Eph. 2:8; Gal. 3:22). The Holy Spirit is the third person of the triune being of God and He is our helper, aider and assistant throughout our Christian journey (John 14:16, 26; 15:26).

Christianity is the only religion that teaches salvation by grace, unlike Orthodox Judaism, which teaches that salvation comes through one's personal obedience to the Laws of the Torah. Accurate definition does not mean full understanding, but it is essential in order to avoid errors that can make it difficult to give a reason for the hope that is within you (1 Peter 3:15). Although the Trinity seems like a vague concept, it can be fully understood. However, due to lack of understanding, the average Christian probably avoids it or improperly discloses its proper definition.

We are instructed in Peter's first epistle to hold the LORD as holy, and be prepared to give an answer concerning why we hold to this hope. If our view of the LORD is incorrect, then naturally our answer of who God is and who He is to us will likely be incorrect. This is in part the purpose of this study.

The concept of the Trinity isn't difficult to understand. In fact, God has uniquely displayed it within creation (Romans 1:20). Consider the chemistry of H_2O and how it can exist in three different forms. This chemical is a perfect reflection of the concept of the Trinity. When we see H_2O in liquid, gas or a solid form, we still understand that it is H_2O. Just because the form or characteristics of H_2O changes doesn't displace its fundamental identity.

Within the Trinity, God is still "One God." In Genesis 1:26 it states, *"And God said, Let us make man in our image, after our likeness: and let them have dominion over the fish of the sea, and over the fowl of the air, and over the cattle, and over all the earth, and over every creeping thing that creepeth upon the earth."* Notice that the Bible does not say, "And the gods said..."

God's statement, "Let us make man," may sound like a contradiction to our prior declaration, but it contextually implies an internal conversation. This may seem like an error in translation or what some call a conversation with angels, but in reality, it is an internal consultation. God within His multiplicity, consults with Himself in order to make mankind. Genesis 3:22 further discusses the "us" concept saying, "*And the LORD God said, Behold, the man is become as one of us, to know good and evil: and now, lest he put forth his hand, and take also of the tree of life, and eat, and live forever.*" These references occur before the reader even gets out of Genesis. **Therefore, we assert that the Trinity is the belief that God is one in being, and three in person.**

GLOBAL CHRISTIANITY

Is devout Christianity as global as many would assume? According to the Pew Research Center's Forum on Religion & Public Life, a report was conducted on the size and distribution of the world's Christian population. Findings consisted of Global Christianity which stated, "*...Christians are diverse theologically as well as geographically, the new study finds. About half are Catholic. Protestants, broadly defined, make up 37%. Orthodox Christians comprise 12% of Christians worldwide. Other Christians, such as Mormons and Jehovah's Witnesses, make up the remaining 1% of the global Christian population.*"

Is Christianity still the largest Religion?

As previously mentioned, the followers of Jesus were first called Christians in Antioch (Acts 11:26), however, there were very controversial beliefs that distinguished them from their close Judaic neighbors? Every religion has a criteria that helps others identify their institutional affiliation or origin.

Within Christianity, there are various credos or doctrines that are "essential" or "cardinal" in order for one to be considered Christian. The Pew Research Center acknowledges that some of the doctrines regarding organized religions within their report deviate from biblical doctrine, however, they still identified them as Christian. While there will probably remain some denominational doctrines that are not essential in order to be Christian, there are others that are fundamental in order for a person to authentically identify himself/herself as Christian. For instance:

1. A Christian will affirm the Holy Bible as the inerrant and infallible Word of God (2 Tim. 3:16-17).
2. A Christian will proclaim Jesus Christ as Lord and Savior, and none other (Acts 11:20; 1 Cor. 3:11; Gal. 1:7-9).
3. A Christian will believe in the death, burial, and resurrection of Jesus (Rom. 10:9).
4. A Christian will live as Jesus commanded (John 13:34-35, 14:15-17; Jas. 2)

Human imperfections do not have to be defended, however, if a professing Christian does not live by Biblical standards, then he/she is not truly Christian. The Bible enforces an exact proclamation and demonstration of true Christian faith in the one true God. However, there are many "Christian" sect that ascribe to various false deities and erroneous doctrines. For example, the god of Mormonism is a deified man from another planet. Jehovah's Witnesses are actually polytheistic believers who separate the deity of Jesus from that of God the Father while denying that God is a Trinity.

Therefore, if the Pew Research Center includes various religions that do not meet the criteria to be called Christian, then is it possible that Christianity is no longer the largest religion in the world? Below is a list of Christian traditions included within the Pew

Research Center's report of the distribution of the world's Christian population:

- **Catholic Church**
- **Protestant** (this report included three groups),[22] **Historic Protestants, and Independent Protestant Christians**[23]
- **Anglicans**
- **Orthodox Christians**
- **Church of Latter-day Saints (Mormons)**
- **Jehovah's Witnesses**: Jehovah's Witnesses believe that "Christ is God's Son and is inferior to Him" as well as that the destruction of the present world system at Armageddon is imminent.[24] They prefer their own Bible translation, the *New World Translation of the Holy Scriptures*.[25]
- **Christian Science Church**: Christian Science was founded by Mary Baker Eddy (1821-1910). Her 1875 book, *Science and Health with Key to the Scriptures*, is one of its central texts, along with the Bible.[26]

Many of these religions depart from biblical Christianity and have supplementary revered texts beyond the Bible, along with their own interpretations of the Christian Bible. With such scrutiny, it is likely that most of the religions that identify themselves as Christian are actually not. Therefore, if our analysis is accurate, then we will likely witness the fulfillment of Jesus' prophecy in vast quantities:

> *"Not every one that saith unto me, Lord, Lord, shall enter into the kingdom of heaven; but he that doeth the will of my Father which is in heaven. 22.Many will say to me in that day, Lord, Lord, have we not prophesied in thy name? Have we not cast out devils? and in thy name done many wonderful works? 23.And then will I profess unto them, I never knew you: depart from me, ye that work iniquity"* (Matt. 7:21-23).

FREEMASONRY

"A BIBLICAL PERSPECTIVE OF FREEMASONRY"

Secret societies have existed throughout the history of mankind. From men possessing secret religious knowledge to men seeking to hide clandestine activity from the public, these societies remain shrouded and covered by the members that support and make up their organizations. Freemasonry is one secret society that is both a local and international religion. Historically, Freemasonry has roots that extend definitively to the times of the Roman Empire, but according to legend this organization is said to have existed at the building of the temple at Jerusalem. Regardless of history or legend, this secret society has proven to be an attractive lure for individuals both unaffiliated with Christianity and in leadership positions within the Christian church. Due to the alluring nature of Freemasonry and secret societies similar to it, it is necessary to examine such organizations in light of God's Word to see if it is proper for a Christian to support such institutions.

Freemasonry

Definition of Freemasonry

The term mason comes from a French word *maszun* which meant "stone craftsman." Freemasonry originated in Britain where men that worked on the church cathedrals between the years of 300 AD to 900 AD were classified as masons.[27] Further clarification of the term separated these craftsmen into two classes; those who handled hard stone ("hard hewers" or "rough masons") and highly skilled cutters of softer, chalky rock ("free stone").[28] These craftsmen became known as the shortened title of freemason.[29]

Historical Background

The history of Freemasonry can be classified in terms of esoteric interpretations and what appears to be more plausible and historically accurate information. The esoteric viewpoint states that freemasonry could have existed at the time of the Tower of Babel or with Moses in his instructions for the tabernacle. However, the most accepted myth regarding the origin of freemasonry aligns with the building of the temple at Jerusalem under the reign of King Solomon. In Second Chronicles chapter two, Solomon contacts Hiram king of Tyre requesting a "foreman" for the building of the temple.

"Send me now therefore a man cunning to work in gold, and in silver, and in brass, and in iron, and in purple, and crimson, and blue, and that can skill to grave with the cunning men that are with me in Judah and in Jerusalem, whom David my father did provide."

~ 2 Chronicles 2:7

According to Masonic legend the man sent to Solomon is named Hiram Abiff.[30] Where the Masonic legend comes in occurs with Hiram's evaluation of when men are ready to receive the "mysteries," which would indicate that they are ready to handle more challenging tasks and responsibilities.[31] Three men coveted such knowledge of mysteries and requested that Hiram give them this information, yet upon refusing their inquiries, the three men devised a plan to kill Hiram as he walked out of the temple under construction.[32] The men, positioned at different doors of the temple, cut Hiram's throat, hit him over the head, and pierce his heart with different masonry tools then fled to different parts of the known globe. Twelve craftsmen, who had backed out of the plot, go to Solomon to reveal the truth of all that happened while wearing white gloves and white aprons to prove their innocence.[33] There is no current historical documentation proving the existence of the three men or Hiram Abiff, yet white gloves and aprons and the masonry tools used to kill Hiram often find their way into Masonic symbology.[34]

A more plausible historical account is based on the information leading up to the establishment of the first Grand Lodge in 1717 AD.[35] Prior to this date, masonry was simply a workers guild or trade union. The secretive nature of the Freemasons was to insure that trade secrets were kept from those seeking the competitive wages the masons receive in their skill with architectural structure. In building cathedrals, bridges, fortifications, and other works of stone, masons brought attention to their skill as builders. However, around the 1500's it appears that non-Masons were allowed to join these organizations once reserved solely for tradesmen. This is partly due to declining membership during the reign of Henry VIII, who stripped the influence of the Church of England and simultaneously the money used by the church to hire masons for projects. This period in Masonic history marks a change from "operative" membership to "speculative" membership, since members began to apply hidden meaning to the tools of masonry and contemplated them in light of the mysteries of life.[36] In accepting non-tradesmen into their ranks, Freemasonry was once again allowed to flourish and maintain its membership.

Freemasonry in light of Christianity

Freemasonry is today more than a trade union or social club. With more than 1.7 million members internationally, Freemasons are a secret society boasting membership in political arenas, pulpits, and famous celebrities and figures worldwide. Having so many influential leaders in its ranks, it begs the question, is Freemasonry in conflict with what the Bible teaches the Christian? In examination of this question, basic tenets of the Christian faith will be used to respond: the nature of God, the exclusiveness of God's Word, and the person of Jesus Christ.

First, in addressing the nature of God, in order to boost membership, it must be stated that Masons do not advocate any one religion. As long as an individual believes in a "Supreme Being," he is readily admitted into the Freemasons. God in context of the Holy Bible is seen as the Supreme Architect, not triune, while in Biblical Christianity, God is one in three persons. This alone is in direct conflict with the beliefs of Christianity. In the Lodge, one is not allowed to discuss religion, politics, news, and so on, yet the fact remains, this understanding is a main tenet and view that a Mason accepts upon undergoing the rituals associated with belonging to such an organization.[37]

Second, the Word of God is seen as one of three "Volumes of Law" and just one of the symbols of God's will for man. Upon acceptance of Masonic procedure, ritual, and doctrine, the Christian readily accepts that God's Word is not the exclusive truth of God given to men through inspiration of the Holy Spirit. Sources of "God's revelatory truth" to a Mason therefore are not sola scriptura, but include the Koran, the Bhagavad-Gita, and the Hindu Vedas. This ideology is in direct contradiction of God's Word and illogical at the same time. For even in a "volume" there should be continuity and underlying structure to the contents of a collection of works. Putting three or more contradictory books together does not make it a volume, but a collection of writings. The Christian choosing to affiliate with Masonic practices readily accepts this ritual as logical while also accepting the teaching of the Koran, Gita, and Vedas as divinely inspired books of God's will.

Last, the person of Jesus Christ is of utmost concern and should be to the Christian. In the "Volumes of Law" discussed previously, the Muslim's Koran and Hindu's Vedas are included. Both teach that Jesus is a moral teacher and not the son of God. In so doing, both books contradict the Christian faith. Islam teaches that Christ did not die on the cross; this alone is a central and vital tenet to the Christian faith (I Corinthians 15). The Vedas teach that eternal salvation is impossible for certain groups of people, while Jesus states that, "God so love the world, that he gave his only begotten Son, that whosoever believeth in him should not perish, but have everlasting life" (John 3:16). This alone is proof enough that the major belief of many Masons is that Jesus is not to be deified or worshipped. The Masons believe that Jesus is no more than a great moral teacher, and no more divine or unique than Buddha or Muhammad. It is therefore the conclusion of the authors that Freemasonry should not be supported by Christians due to its nullification of God's true nature, the exclusivity of the Bible as God's inspired Word, and work and deity of Jesus Christ.

Conclusion

Several places in the Scriptures address coming out of darkness. When an individual that professes Christ as Lord and Savior aligns himself with an organization that identifies or has been identified as secret, one must ask why such an organization is deemed to be secret. Secret societies that boast secret knowledge or are steeped in clandestine activity alone should alarm the Bible believing

Christian. Unfortunately, many people join such organizations for the sake of companionship, prestige, or legacy alignment.

Freemasons are by no means a Christian organization, nor do they advocate the central tenets of Christian faith. Apart from the points addressed, Freemasonry is steeped in ritual and symbolism that ultimately denounce Christ and elevate the Lodge above the place of the one true God. Hopefully the points addressed in the preceding paragraphs will shed light upon why Freemasonry is not to be supported by Christians. As children of light, the Word of God admonishes each believer to walk in the light as he is in the light that we may have fellowship one with another (I John 1:7). In order to walk in the light, we must fully embrace the teaching delivered to us through Jesus Christ, accepting Him as the Son of God, and the Word He speaks as spirit and life (John 6:63).

Notes

ISLAM

Islam is a monotheistic religion articulated by an Arab named Muhammad ibn `Abd Allah (simply known as Muhammad). Islam is at this time one of the world's fastest growing religions. There are over 1.5 billion Muslims, that's over 20 percent of the world's population, making Islam the world's second-largest religion after Christianity.

HISTORICAL BACKGROUND

Muhammad lived between 570 AD – June 8, 632 AD. As legend would have it, Muhammad began receiving divine messages from the angel Gabriel, which told him to recite. These recitations became part of the book now called the Qur'an. The Qur'an or Koran is the central religious text of Islam and is believed by its adherents (called Muslims) to be the word for word proclamation of God (Allah).

The Qur'an is arranged in 114 *surah's* (Qur'anic chapters). A surah is better known in the West as a chapter in the English translation (Surah 2:23). Surah's are numbered consecutively and each surah consist of ayats or verses. For example, Surah 1 contains 7 ayats, and Surah 2 contains 286 ayats. The Qur'an does not serve as the only source of reference. Aside from the Qur'an, some Muslim sources of study include the Hadith (which are Muhammad's sayings or a report about the conduct of his life), then there is the *sira* or *sirah* (pronounced as *seera*) which is the biography of Muhammad.

Muslims also believe that Islam is the only faith that has been previously revealed through ordinary prophets such as Adam, Noah, Abraham, Moses, and Jesus. However, followers of orthodox Islam accept that Jesus Christ was born of a virgin, lived a perfect life, performed miracles, is an integral prophet in Islam that will fight with the Mahdi against the Anti-Christ. Contrary to the Christian Scriptures, Muslims believe that he was not crucified, but translated into paradise. Some Muslims have even been quoted as saying that "Jesus is the Messiah!" The Qur'an also affirms that Jesus is the Messiah (Surah 3:45). As a matter of fact, Jesus is quoted in Qur'anic scripture more than the prophet Muhammad and said to be the seal (highest ranking) of the prophets of Islam, of which there are approximately 300,000. Muslims do not believe in salvation through Jesus Christ.

Believers and non-Believers

Initially, Muhammad spoke positively about Jews and Christians, but, as time progressed, so did his defiance toward Bible-based Christianity. According to the Qur'an, Muslim believers are commanded not to befriend Jews or Christians (Surah 5:51).

Additionally, Muslim's are commanded to fight against those who do not believe in Allah. Those that do not embrace the Islamic faith when conquered are required to pay the Jizyah (the commutation tax) and are to be compliant to Sharia law (Surah 9:29). In the name of Allah, Muhammad goes on to call Christians polytheist because of their belief in the Trinity. Surah 9:30 states, "And the Jews say: 'Uzair (Ezra) is the son of Allah, and the Christians say: Messiah (i.e. Jesus Christ) is the son of Allah. That is a saying from their mouths. They imitate the saying of the disbelievers of old. Allah's curse be on them, how they are deluded away from the truth!"

It is important to understand how true followers of traditional Islam view non-Muslims or disbelievers. The term disbeliever within Islam derives from the Arabic word *kafir*. This term is pluralistic in meaning because it carries within it the context of an enemy of Allah (Surah 8:12; 9:5, 29; 47:4). This term is also synonymous with polytheists (Surah 9:5), idolaters, Christians, Jews, and other non-adherents to Islam. Essentially, anyone that does not regard or submit to the teachings of Muhammad are kafirs (enemies to Allah's cause).

THE FIVE PILLARS OF ISLAM

The Five Pillars of Islam arkān al-Islām, أركان الإسلام are five basic performance mandates in Islam, and are the foundation of Muslim life. These Five Pillars are summarized in the hadith of Gabriel:

1. *Shahadah* – The Islamic declaration of faith consist of an Arabic saying, "La ilaha illa Allah, Muhammadur rasoolu Allah." This saying means, "There is no true god but God (Allah), and Muhammad is his Prophet." Similar to Christianity, the shahadah is the Muslim's declaration of salvation.

2. *Salat* – Muslims are required to perform five prayers a day, all under a few minutes each. Prayers are performed at dawn, noon,

mid-afternoon, sunset, and night. There are no restrictions regarding where a Muslim may pray.

3. *Zakāt* – Charities; a mandatory giving of a specified percent of ones income in countries with shariah law. Many Islamist will lead you to believe that zakāt serves solely to address the needs of the impoverished, however, it is believed that zakāt may be allocated toward the ransom of captive Muslims and the support of jihad.

- "As-Sadaqat (here it means zakat) are only for the fuqara (poor), and al-masakin (the poor) and those employed to collect (the funds); and for to attract the hearts of those who have been inclined (towards Islam); and to free the captives; and for those in debt; and for Allah's cause (for example, mujahidun – those fighting in the holy wars), and for the wayfarer (a traveler who is cut off from everything); a duty imposed by Allah. And Allah is All-Knowing, All-Wise." ~ Surah 9:60

- They [the infidels] would like you to reject the faith [of Islam] as they have done themselves, that you may be all alike; therefore, make no friends with them until they emigrate in the cause of Allah. But if they turn back (to hostility), then capture them and kill them wherever you find them, and do not take any one of them as a friend or as a helper. ~ Surah 4:89

- But when the prohibited (four) months (when no attack on the breakers of the treaties was permissible) have expired, slay such polytheists (who broke their treaties) wherever you find them and capture them and besiege them and lie in wait for them in every place from which it is possible to perceive the enemy and watch their movements. But if they turn in repentance and keep up prayer and go on presenting the zakat, leave their path free. Indeed, Allah is great protector, ever merciful. ~ Surah 9:5

Hopefully, those verses help clarify *"the cause of Allah"* according to the words of Muhammad himself. The cause of Allah is not one of peace, but of intimidation, violence and hostility toward non-Muslims. A deeper look into the Qur'anic scriptures will reveal that Allah is quite the opposite of love and redemption.

4. *Ramadan* or *Sawm* – the ninth month of the Islamic calendar and the month of fasting for all Muslims. The month is spent fasting during the light of day from sunrise to sunset.

5. *Hajj:* An annual pilgrimage to Mecca, and a religious mandate for Muslims to be carried out at least once in their lifetime by all adult Muslims who are capable to undertake the journey. This also means that each Muslim taking the journey must be able to support their family during their absence.

WHAT IS JIHAD?

After a thorough analysis of jihad, we also rank it among the Five Pillars of Islam. Many Muslims intentionally mislead kafirs (non-Muslims) into believing that jihad is peaceful in origin, but it is not. The Muslim sect of the Kharijites, who interpret jihad as holy warfare, have elevated it to the ranks of the Five Pillars of Islam—making it a Sixth Pillars or essential religious practice for a Muslim. This is the exact doctrine that is often seen within Muslim terrorist groups. They use Muhammad's concepts within the Qur'an and Hadith to execute his teachings of killing and subjugating kafirs. The second interpretation of jihad is professed by many passive Muslims to advocate peace. This division in how Muslims view jihad is a figurative, internal, and personal spiritual struggle against evil. We consider this reformed concept of jihad to be subordinate to Muhammad's original framework of its purpose and meaning.

The Doctrine of Jihad According to the Qur'an

From a Westerner's perspective, the Qur'an may appear to be mysterious and difficult to understand; however, modern translations enable the modern reader to decipher through the text to accurately grasp the core beliefs within Islam. Unfortunately, there are some translations that have softened Muhammad's harsh and hostile remarks toward kafirs in order to make Islam seem more appealing.

For the Muslim, the Qur'an is the most sacred and eternal commands of Allah. The teachings of Jihad are an essential message within the Qur'an. The following excerpts from the Qur'an will help highlight the true doctrine concerning "the cause of Allah [Jihad]."

1. "And fight in the Way of Allah those who fight you, but transgress not the limits. Truly, Allah likes not the transgressors. [This verse is the first one revealed in connection with jihad, but was supplemented by another (V.9:36)]. [191.] And kill them wherever you find them, and turn them out from where they have turned you out. And Al-Fitnah is worse than killing. And fight not with them at Al-Masjid-al-Haram (the sanctuary at Makkah), unless they (first) fight you there. But if they attack you, then kill them. Such is the recompense of the disbelievers. [192.] But if they cease, then Allah is Oft -Forgiving, Most Merciful. [193.] And fight them until there is no more Fitnah (disbelief and worshipping of others along with Allah) and (all and every kind of) worship is for Allah (Alone). But if they cease, let there be no transgression except against Az-Zalimun

(the polytheists, and wrong-doers, etc.)." ~ Surah 2:190-193

2. Those who believe, fight in the Cause of Allah, and those who disbelieve, fight in the cause of Taghut (Satan, etc.). So fight you against the friends of Shaitan (Satan); Ever feeble indeed is the plot of Shaitan (Satan). ~ Surah 4:76

3. "O you who believe! What is the matter with you, that when you are asked to march forth in the Cause of Allah (i.e. Jihad) you cling heavily to the earth? Are you pleased with the life of this world rather than the Hereafter? But little is the enjoyment of the life of this world as compared with the Hereafter. [39.] If you march not forth, He will punish you with a painful torment and will replace you by another people, and you cannot harm Him at all, and Allah is Able to do all things. ~ Surah 9:38-39

4. "Verily, Allah loves those who fight in His Cause in rows (ranks) as if they were a solid structure." ~ Surah 61:4 (Also see Surah 61:10-12.)

The Doctrine of Jihad According to the Hadith

The Hadith comprises literary collections of the sayings and accounts of Muhammad's life. Below are a collection of Hadith's of Muhammad regarding Jihad. The teachings of Jihad are an essential message within the Hadith. The following Hadith's will help highlight the true doctrine concerning "the cause of Allah [Jihad]."

1. "The Prophet said, "The person who participates in (Holy battles) in Allah's cause and nothing compels him to do so except belief in Allah and His Apostles, will be recompensed by Allah either with a reward, or booty (if he survives) or will

be admitted to Paradise (if he is killed in the battle as a martyr). Had I not found it difficult for my followers, then I would not remain behind any sariya going for Jihad and I would have loved to be martyred in Allah's cause and then made alive, and then martyred and then made alive, and then again martyred in His cause" (Volume 1, Book 2, Number 35, Narrated Abu Huraira).

2. A man came to Allah's Apostle and said, "Instruct me as to such a deed as equals jihad (in reward)." He replied, "I do not find such a deed." Then he added, "Can you, while the Muslim fighter is in the battle-field, enter your mosque to perform prayers without ceasing and fast and never break your fast?" The man said, "But who can do that?" Abu- Huraira added, "The Mujahid (i.e. Muslim fighter) is rewarded even for the footsteps of his horse while it wanders bout (for grazing) tied in a long rope." (Volume 4, Book 52, Number 44: Narrated Abu Huraira).

Within the above text, Muhammad in his own words according to Abu Huraira compares jihad to "the Muslim fighter in the battle-field." Within Hadith's such as these, there are no clearer indicators concerning the true context of jihad.

3. Um Haram said, "Once the Prophet slept in my house near to me and got up smiling. I said, 'What makes you smile?' He replied, 'Some of my followers who (i.e. in a dream) were presented to me sailing on this green sea like kings on thrones.' I said, 'O Allah's Apostle! Invoke Allah to make me one of them." So the Prophet invoked Allah for her and went to sleep again. He did the same (i.e. got up and told his dream) and Um Haran repeated her question and he gave the same reply. She said, "Invoke Allah to make me one of them." He

said, "You are among the first batch." Later on it happened that she went out in the company of her husband 'Ubada bin As-Samit who went for jihad and it was the first time the Muslims undertook a naval expedition led by Mu Awiya. When the expedition came to an end and they were returning to Sham, a riding animal was presented to her to ride, but the animal let her fall and thus she died. (Volume 4, Book 52, Number 44: Narrated Abu Huraira).

If jihad is an internal struggle with oneself to get closer to Allah, then why would any Muslim of Muhammad's time need to go out on any expeditions? Especially a naval expedition. Muhammad permitted Um Haram, the wife of 'Ubada bin As-Samit to fight in jihad as a Mujahid (i.e. Muslim fighter). However, when asked about jihad by his own wives, this was Muhammad's reply, "The mother of the faithful believers, I requested the Prophet permit me to participate in jihad, but he said, "Your jihad is the performance of hajj. The mother of the faithful believers: The Prophet was asked by his wives about the jihad and he replied, "The best jihad (for you) is (the performance of) Hajj" (Volume 4, Book 52, Number 127-128).

4. "Allah's Apostle said, "Allah guarantees (the person who carries out jihad in His Cause and nothing compelled him to go out but jihad in His Cause and the belief in His Word) that He will either admit him into Paradise (Martyrdom) or return him with reward or booty he has earned to his residence from where he went out" (Volume 9, Book 93, Number 555: Narrated Abu Huraira).

In reality, jihad is pluralistic, meaning it consist of two or more elements, therefore, no distinctions exist within jihad. Historically, whenever Islam was not the dominating force within a region, the true expression of jihad was suppressed and the "peaceful" religion of Islam became its facade. Within the parameters of the culture of Islam (i.e. believer to believer), jihad will become representative of "the internal battle against the self and the struggle to overcome one's egotism in order to be closer to Allah." Conversely, outside of the parameters of the culture of Islam (i.e. believer to kafir), Jihad becomes offensive in nature. "And fight them until there is no more fitnah (disbelief and worshipping of others along with Allah) and (all and every kind of) worship is for Allah (Alone). But if they cease, let there be no transgression except against Az-Zalimun (the polytheists, and wrong-doers, etc.) (Surah 2:193)." When Islam begins to gain political momentum and Sharia gains power, then the true agenda of Islam becomes increasingly offensive.

The False Dichotomy of Islam

The controversy over the meaning of jihad or Islamic doctrine is not within the vantage point of the kafir, it is within Islam itself. Conversely, the true essence of jihad is evident within the westerner's categorization of those that are active within extremism. The mainstream media, sympathizers, and supporters of Islam often craft an illusion of moderate ("good") Muslims vs. extremist ("evil") Muslims. The tendency to categorize Muslims has been indoctrinated within the thinking of Western Muslim scholars, and advocates of Islam. This false dichotomy is the primary reason why the ideology and creed of Islam is thought to be a religion of peace. To be a true Muslim, one must solemnly adhere to the ideologies of Islam. To deny or ignore even one of the Qur'anic commands is to deny Islam itself. As a result, that individual can never truly be an accurate representative of Islam, unless he or she completely embraces and adheres to its article of faith.

To identify Muslims as moderate or extremist is misleading, especially when the fundamental doctrine of the Qur'an advocates war, inequality, violence, murder, and the maltreatment of others.

COMPARING THE QUR'AN WITH THE BIBLE
Teachings about God

The Qur'an teaches:	*The Bible teaches:*
1. There is one God (Allah) – Surah 3:64	1. There is one God – 1 Cor. 8:6
2. Allah is all powerful – Surah 2:106	2. God is all powerful – Heb. 1:3
3. To reject the concept of the Trinity – Surah 61:7; 77:29	3. The Godhead is composed of three distinct substance). – cf. John 1:1-5; Phil. 2:5-8; 2 John 9; Matt. 28:19
4. Allah is all-knowing and wise – Surah 24:21-22	4. God is all-knowing – Heb. 4:13; Rom. 16:27
5. Allah is the creator of the Universe – Surah 41:9-12	5. God is the creator of all things – Gen. 1:1; John 1:1-4

War and Vengeance

The Qur'an:	*The Bible:*
1. Allows war and vengeance for self-defense against persecution – Surah 8:59-60	1. Forbids war and vengeance when persecuted for righteousness' sake – Matt. 5:10 -12,38-48
2. Allows use of war in promoting the faith against unbelievers and idolaters – Surah 8:65; 9:29	2. Forbids use of war to promote the cause of Christ and the gospel – 2 Cor. 10:3-5

Teachings about Jesus

The Qur'an:	*The Bible:*
1. Considers Jesus a prophet, like Noah, Abraham, Moses (and Muhammad) – Surah 3:84	1. Declares that Jesus is the Christ, the Son of God – Matt. 16:13-18
2. Rejects the divinity of Jesus, denies his preexistence – Surah 4:171	2. Teaches the preexistence of Christ – John 1:1-5, 10; Cor. 1:16-17
3. Believes in the virgin birth, however, teaches that there was no death, burial or resurrection of Jesus – Surah 4:157	3. Proclaims that Jesus died on the cross for our sins, and was raised from the dead – Rom. 10:9-10

Teachings about Salvation

The Qur'an teaches:	*The Bible teaches:*
1. Salvation comes by works – Surah 5:69	1. Salvation is by grace through an obedient faith – Eph. 2:8-9; Tim. 3:4-7
2. Personal righteousness is weighed against personal sin, whichever is greater determines salvation – Surah 23:101-103	2. Jesus died on the cross as atonement for our sins – Rom. 3:21-26
3. A Muslim can be forgiven by repenting of sin – Surah 39:53-54	3. He is the source of eternal salvation to all who obey Him – Heb. 5:9
4. One becomes a Muslim by: Confessing "There is no other god but God; and	4. One becomes a Christian by: a. Believing that Christ died for your sins – John 8:24; Rom. 10:9

4. Muhammad is the Prophet of God" (la ilaha ill'Allah, Muhammad rasul Allah) from the heart.

    b. Repenting of your sins - Acts 2:38; 17:30-31

    c. Confessing your faith in Jesus as the Christ, the Son of God – Matt. 10:32-33; Rom. 10:9-10

Eternal Judgment

The Qur'an teaches:	*The Bible teaches:*
1. Resurrection of the dead and judgment at the Last Day	1. Resurrection of the dead and judgment at the Last Day
2. Paradise for the faithful, served by beautiful virgins – Surah 56:1-38	2. An eternal City, New Jerusalem, in the new heavens and new earth for those whose name is in the Lamb's book of life – Rev. 21:1-7, 9-27; 22:1-5
3. Hell for unbelievers, with eternal torment – Surah 56:39-56	3. The lake of fire for the unbelieving and wicked – Rev. 20:15; 21:8

Additionally, when the sayings and endeavors of their founder Muhammad advocated war on non-believers, and when we witness the oppression of Sharia legislated upon non-Muslims, it is evident that there has and will always existed a brokenness within the core beliefs of Islamic doctrine.

The Word of God

The Qur'an:	The Bible teaches:
1. Validates 4 inspired books – the *Torah* (5 books of Moses), *Zabur* (the Psalms), *Injil* (the Gospel), and the *Qur'an* a. The first three have been corrupted; the Qur'an provides the final revelation of God's Word	1. Old and New Testaments, which contain the revelation of God's Word – 2 Tim. 3:16-17 2. God's Word cannot be corrupted, but is preserved – 1 Pet. 1:23-25; Matt. 24:35; Isa. 40:8 3. Revelation of God's Word is fully and finally revealed – 2 Pet. 1:3; Jude 3

Prayer, Fasting, and Worship

The Qur'an:	The Bible:
1. Has set times to offer prayers (five times per day) 2. Has set periods and procedures in which to fast (the month of Ramadan) 3. Places emphasis on ceremonial rituals such as washings, posture in prayer	1. Calls for fervent and steadfast prayer, with no set times proscribed – 1 Thess. 5:17; Cor. 4:2 2. Has a place for fasting, but left up to the individual – Matt. 6:16-18; Acts 13:2-3; 14:23 3. Places emphasis upon the spiritual aspect of worship – John 4:23-24; Eph. 5:19; Cor. 3:16

Islam

Morals

The Qur'an:	The Bible:
1. Forbids alcohol, gambling – Surah 5:93-94	1. Forbids drunkenness, covetousness, and other "works of the flesh" – Gal. 5:19-21
2. Forbids eating pork	
3. Allows up to four wives, may divorce and remarry them twice – Surah 2:229	2. Allows all foods with thanksgiving and prayer – 1 Tim. 4:4-5
	3. Teaches monogamy, divorce only for fornication – Matt. 19:9; 1 Cor. 7:2

Treatment of Women

The Qur'an teaches:	The Bible teaches:
1. Men have more rights than women – Surah 2:228	1. Men and women are fellow heirs of the grace of life – 1 Pet. 3:7; Gal. 3:28-29
2. Women do not attend public prayers at the Mosque	2. Women do not have leadership roles in the church – 1 Cor. 11:3; 14:34-37; 2 Tim. 2:11-12
3. A husband may punish a wife, but not before cautioning her. However, if he deems her conduct unsuitable, he is instructed to refuse to share the same bed with her and beat her. – Surah 4:34	3. A husband is forbidden from withholding what is due to his wife and is required to treat her with love, tenderness, and understanding, along with sacrificing himself on behave of his wife. – 1 Cor. 7:3-5; Eph. 5:2; 1 Pet. 3:7

When witnessing to Muslims, the Christian apologist should:

1. **Avoid the assumption that Muslims have the same contextual usage.** When the Christian says God, they mean the God of the Bible, and the incarnation of Jesus Christ, the Messiah. However, when Muslims say God, they mean Allah. The only true God of the Bible is vastly different from the deity of the Qur'an. That is why contextual accuracy is essential when witnessing to Muslims.

2. **Be familiar with the Islamic worldview.** We strongly encourage Christians to have a suitable knowledge base of the Islamic faith in order to effectively reach them. A deficit knowledge base of any denomination or faith handicaps the Christian at a disadvantage and could potentially do more harm than good. Therefore, we encourage all Christians to have a basic knowledge of the Islamic faith in order to properly witness to the Muslim (2 Tim. 2:15; 1 Peter 3:15-16).

3. **Avoid harsh criticisms of the Qur'an.** There is nothing more offensive and repelling to a non-believer than for someone to mock something that they passionately believe in. Paul said, "Brethren, if a man be overtaken in a fault, ye which are spiritual, restore such an one in the spirit of meekness (kindness); considering thyself, lest thou also be tempted" (Gal. 6:1). Notice how Paul didn't say, "Brethren, if a brethren be overtaken..." Therefore, this verse applies not only to those within the assembly of believers, but also to those outside of the Christian faith. Thus, we must extend kind words of edification also to non-Christians.

4. **Avoid politically charged subjects.** We can clearly see the controversy within politically charged subjects through

the discourse of the Pharisees, Sadducees, and Scribes of Biblical times. Oftentimes, these individuals would present politically charged questions in an effort to trap or discredit Jesus (Matt. 22:15-22). Conversely, Jesus always managed to extinguish the fiery darts of controversial remarks and inquiries. Worldly politics have very little, if anything to do with the kingdom of God. The Jewish community of Jesus' day assumed that the purpose of the Messiah was to establish a new government and political arena, however, that's not why Jesus came and He made that apparent. Whenever Jesus referred to the Kingdom of God, it was always connected to repentance and salvation of people, not a worldly system. Politics is about the order of worldly systems and its survival, not the salvation of all people.

5. **Preach Jesus and nothing else.** It's important to avoid getting into theological sparing matches whenever possible. Sharing Jesus Christ is not about showboating your knowledge of the Bible or about reprimanding another in subjugation to the Bible, but about genuinely connecting with the recipient and coaching them toward the validity and truthfulness of the entire Bible. Some zealously jump at the opportunity to exercise their knowledge by challenging those of opposing faiths, but this should not be the temperament of the Christian. Our apologetic endeavors are to promote Jesus Christ and the defense of the message of the Gospel, not the advancement of one's own agenda or ego at the expense of courtesy and respect toward others (Matt. 10:14; Col. 3:1-4).

Since Muslims believe that there is some validity within the Torah and Injil (Gospel) as far as they are correct in relation to the Qur'an (Surah 9:111), the Christian should use these documents to his or her advantage. Since Muslims are not sure about their final state (Surah 46:9), use what is known from the Scriptures concerning the final state of humanity to give hope about heaven and the New Earth. An Apologist seeking to win a Muslim to Christ must be led by the Spirit of God in order to reach them for the kingdom. The love that Christ showed on Calvary's cross must be exhibited in the life, conduct and speech of a Christian. This key is the true drawing power for a non-Christian of any religion (Cor. 4:3; Gal. 3:7-10; Eph. 2:8; John 3:16).

"The teaching of Jesus is clear. No one ought to be compelled to become a Christian. This sets the Christian faith drastically apart from Islam. In no country where the Christian faith is the faith of the majority is it illegal to propagate another faith. There is no country in the world that I know of where the renunciation of one's Christian faith puts one in danger of being hunted down by the powers of the state. Yet, there are numerous Islamic countries where it is against the law to publicly proclaim the gospel of Jesus Christ, and where a Muslim who renounces his or her belief in Islam to believe in anything else risks death. Freedom to critique the text of the Koran and the person of Mohammed are prohibited by the laws of blasphemy, and the result is torturous punishment. One must respect the concern of a culture to protect what it deems sacred, but to compel a belief in Jesus Christ is foreign to the gospel, and that is a vital difference. The contrast is all too clear."

~ Ravi Zacharias

Jesus Among Other Gods & Deliver Us from Evil

QUICK REFERENCE GUIDE

1. No one can change Allah's words – Surah 18:27

2. The Qur'an is perfect – Surah 5:49

3. There is only one God (Allah) – Surah 3:64

4. Allah is the creator of the Universe – Surah 41:9-12

5. Allah is not a Trinity

6. Allah is Father to no one – Surah 5:18; 19:88-93; 21:26

7. Allah does not love unbelievers – Surah 3:32

8. Jesus was born of a virgin – Surah 3:47

9. Jesus performed many miracles (i.e. healing the blind, leprous, and raised the dead) – Surah 3:49

10. Jesus was the Messiah – Surah 3:45

11. Jesus was not divine – Surah 5:75; 5:116-117

12. Jesus did not die on the cross – Surah 4:157

13. Jesus was taken by Allah into his presence – Surah 4:158

14. Christians are the nearest in friendship to Muslims – Surah 5:82

15. Christians have scriptures from God – Surah 5:68; 7:157

16. Christians are to be fought and subdued – Surah 9:29

17. Christians who are unbelievers that do not believe in Allah are the worst creatures – Surah 98:6

18. Salvation by righteous deeds – Surah 5:69

19. The Torah and the Gospel are God's inspired word – Surah 3:3-4

20. Muslims must not befriend Christians—for a Muslim to become a collaborator with an unbelieving Jew or Christian is to become one of them – Surah 5:51

21. Muslims are instructed to kill unbelievers – Surah 9:5; 47:4

22. Muslims are instructed to kill those that commit apostasy

23. The Qur'an is free from error – Surah 4:82

NATION OF ISLAM

"THE DOCTRINE OF WALLACE D. FARD"

The Nation of Islam (NOI) was created by Wallace D. Fard, also known as Wallace Fard Muhammad. Fard claimed to come from the Islamic city of Mecca. He began a mosque in Detroit in 1930. He taught that Christianity should be rejected since it was the "slave-master's religion." In 1934, Fard disappeared and was neither seen nor heard from again. Fard was succeeded by Elijah Muhammad (Elijah Poole). Elijah Poole was born in Sandersville, Ga. on October 7, 1898. He changed his name to Elijah Muhammad after joining the NOI. After Fard disappeared, Elijah took over the leadership of the NOI.

Malcolm Little was born in 1925. He joined the NOI and changed his name to Malcolm X. He achieved fame in the early 1960s as the spokesperson for Elijah Muhammad. Malcolm X was removed as spokesperson because of an inappropriate remark about the assassination of President Kennedy and was severed from the NOI because of his accusations of sexual misconduct between Elijah Muhammad and female staff members.[38] After he left the NOI, Malcolm began the Muslim Mosque, Inc., in 1964. Less than one year later, on February 21, 1965, Malcolm X was killed by assassins.

Warith Deen Muhammad became the new leader of the NOI after his father, Elijah Muhammad, died on February 25, 1975. Warith eliminated teachings from the NOI that Fard was Allah. Warith led the NOI to adopt beliefs compatible with traditional Islam. He changed the name from the NOI to the World Community of Islam. Later, he altered the name to the American Muslim Mission, but eventually disbanded the organization and his followers became part of traditional Islam. The NOI was resurrected by Louis Farrakhan.

Farrakhan was born Louis Eugene Walcott in New York City on May 11, 1933. He attended college for two years in North Carolina, but left to begin a career as an entertainer. He sang in nightclubs until he joined the NOI. Louis Farrakhan separated from Warith Deen Muhammad in 1978 because of doctrinal disagreements. Farrakhan formed a splinter group using the original name—the Nation of Islam. He reestablished the teachings of Elijah Muhammad and also reinstated the movement's security force known as the Fruit of Islam (FOI). The Nation of Islam does not release statistics, but there are an estimated 25,000 to 100,000 members. Many more people admire Louis Farrakhan as a national leader. In 1995 he called for a Million Man March and several hundred thousand men answered his call.

DOCTRINE

Several teachings of the NOI are incompatible with Christianity. Many of their beliefs are also incompatible with traditional Islam.

God According to the Nation of Islam

The Nation of Islam claims that God is a man. "God is a man and we just cannot make Him other than man."[39] The NOI teaches that Fard was Allah in physical form.[40] According to Elijah Muhammad, Fard told him, "My name is Mahdi; I am God."[41] The NOI continues to teach that Fard is Allah. The current NOI statement is published in every issue of their weekly newspaper, The Final Call, in an article titled "What the Muslims Believe." It states,

> *"12. WE BELIEVE that Allah (God) appeared in the Person of Master W. Fard Muhammad, July, 1930; the long-awaited 'Messiah' of the Christians and the 'Mahdi' of the Muslims."*

The NOI denies that God is spirit. The NOI claims that Christians worship an "invisible spook somewhere in space."[42] According to Elijah Muhammad, "God is in person, and stop looking for a dead Jesus for help, but pray to Him whom Jesus prophesied would come after Him. He who is alive and not a spook."[43]

- *Christian Response*: The Bible teaches that God is spirit (see John 4:24) and denies that He is a man (see Num. 23:19). The NOI worships a false god. Jesus is the only begotten Son of God (see John 3:16). Jesus is unique; there are no other incarnations of God. Jesus, not Fard, is the true Savior of the world (see Acts 4:12; John 1:1-14).

Humanity according to the Nation of Islam

The NOI teaches that blacks are gods and whites are demons. The NOI claims that blacks are of the same race as God. According to Elijah Muhammad, "To accept your own means yourself and your kind, your God Who is of you and you are of Him. It was your fathers who created the heavens and the earth, while there is nothing that the white man has created independently. He did not even create himself. The Black Nation is self-created, while the white race is made by one of the gods and scientists of the Black Nation."[44] The NOI claims that one of these black scientists created the moon. They teach that 66 trillion years ago, he decided to destroy the earth. He drilled a shaft into the earth, filled it with high explosives, and then set it off. He failed to totally destroy the earth but he did blow it into two parts. The smaller part became what we now call the moon.[45]

According to the NOI, a black scientist named Yakub created the white race about 6,000 years ago. They claim that whites are a race of devils.[46] According to Elijah Muhammad, "If you understand it [the Bible] right, you will agree with me that the whole Caucasian race is a race of devils.[47] The NOI claims that Christianity is the devil's religion and was created to mislead blacks.[48]

- *Christian Response:* Blacks are not gods and whites are not demons. Both races are descended from Adam and made in the image of God. "And God said, Let us make man in our image, after our likeness: and let them have dominion over the fish of the sea, and over the fowl or the air, and over the cattle and over all the earth, and over every creeping thing that creepeth upon the earth" (Gen. 1:26). "God created the heaven and the earth" (Gen. 1:1). The moon was created by the God of the Bible, not by a scientist 66 trillion years ago (see Gen. 1:16). The Bible warns Christians not to believe cunningly devised fables (see 2 Pet. 1:16).

The Bible

While the NOI often refers to the Bible, they claim it has been corrupted. "The original scripture called 'The Torah'--revealed to Musa (Moses)--was Holy until the Jews and the Christian scholars started tampering with it."[49] Elijah Muhammad taught, "The Bible is not all holy, nor is it all the word of God!"[50] Contrary to traditional Islam, the NOI also teaches that the Qur'an has been tampered with. "The enemy has tampered with the truth of both books: for he has been permitted to handle both books."[51]

- *Christian Response:* There is no evidence that the Bible has been corrupted as the NOI claims. Jesus promised, "I tell you the truth, until heaven and earth disappear, not the smallest letter, not the least stroke of a pen, will by any means disappear from the Law until everything is accomplished" (Matt. 5:18, NIV). There are thousands of biblical manuscripts that support the Bible as being incorrupt.

The Resurrection

The NOI denies the physical resurrection of the dead. Their doctrinal statement proclaims, "WE BELIEVE in the resurrection of the dead-not in physical resurrection- but in mental resurrection; therefore, they will be resurrected first."[52] Despite their denial of a physical resurrection, the NOI apparently believes that Elijah Muhammad is still alive. Every issue of their newspaper carries a statement of *The Muslim Program.* Included with this statement is Elijah Muhammad's picture and the declaration, "He Lives."

- *Christian Response:* The Bible declares the physical resurrection of the dead (see Ps. 49:15; 71:20; Hos. 13:14; John 5:25; 6:40; 11:25; 2 Cor. 4:14). The dead will rise from the grave. The saved will live forever with the Lord in heaven. The lost will go to hell, a place of everlasting punishment (see Matt. 18:8-9; 25:41-46; Mark 9:43-48).

The Last Judgment

The NOI teaches that a giant spaceship--the Mother Plane-- will carry out Allah's judgment. Black scientists will use the same bombs that brought up the "mountains out of the earth" to destroy the white race.[53] They claim this judgment will not only destroy the white race but also Christianity. Elijah Muhammad asserted, "Armageddon has started, and after it there will be no Christian religion or churches. Jesus was a Muslim, not a Christian."[54] Louis Farrakhan claims that he was taken aboard the Mother Plane in a vision. While in the giant UFO, he spoke to Elijah Muhammad who had been dead for several years.[55] Farrakhan also asserts that this giant spaceship follows him when he travels.[56]

- *Christian Response:* God, not a giant spaceship, will deliver the last judgment upon the world (see Matt. 25:31- 32; 2 Cor. 5:10). God's judgment will not be restricted to one race, but will fall upon all who have not trusted in Jesus Christ as their Lord and Savior (see John 3:18).

Witnessing to People in the NOI

1. Learn the primary Christian truths about God, Christ, the Scripture, and salvation. Know what you believe and why you believe it.

2. Acquaint yourself with the teachings and arguments of the NOI and be ready to give a Christian response (see 1 Pet. 3:15).

3. Listen to those in the NOI and discover why they joined.

4. Explain why you believe the Bible. If they claim that the Bible has been changed, ask them, "When did this happen?" and "What evidence causes you to believe the Bible has been corrupted?"

5. Define your words. Remember that the NOI redefines

many terms. For example, when the NOI talks about God, they mean something very different from the God of the Bible.

6. Tell how to become a Christian. Share your testimony about how Jesus has saved you, and the difference He makes in your life. Center your witness on Christ and how to have a personal relationship with Him. Many NOI followers know about Christianity, but they do not know Christ.

Notes

FIVE PERCENTERS

"NATION OF GODS AND EARTHS"

The Five Percent began as an offshoot of the NOI (Nation of Islam) back in 1964 by Clarence 13X who was a minister in Mosque no. 7 under the tutelege of Malcolm X. The movement was started because Clarence 13X rejected the notion that Wallace Fard was God Incarnate (see NO). He began teaching that the black man himself was god. Five Percenters also depart from NOI in their teaching of the Supreme Alphabet and Supreme Mathematic, an arcane system devised by Clarence 13X wherein each letter or numeral denotes a concept with an accompanying parable. "A" stands for Allah, "B" is Be or Born, "C" is See and so on. This process is known as "dropping science". Supreme Mathematics - teaches that numbers 0-9 means:

1 - Knowledge
2 - Wisdom
3 - Understanding

4 - Culture/Freedom

5 - Power/Refinement

6 - Equality

7 - God

8 - Build/Destroy

9 - Born

0 – Cipher

DOCTRINE

1. Why do they call themselves members of the Nation of Gods and Earths or Five Percenters?

Clarence 13X taught that eighty-five percent of the population is made up of ignorant, unlearned and uncivilized people who need to be led (mostly churchgoers). This eighty-five percent are believed to have no "knowledge of self". Ten percent of the population have *some* knowledge of self [i.e. the real truth], however, they use this knowledge to wield control over the eighty-five percent vs. "liberating" them [most Baptist preachers, including Rev. Jesse Jackson are believed to be in this category]. Lastly, he considered the remaining five percent to be those who thought/believed like himself and his followers. The "poor, righteous teachers", the ones who *do* possess knowledge of themselves, their origins, and the way the world system *really* is -- and additionally, the way in which the New World Order will come about. Their job/mission is to educate the eighty-five percent to what this hidden or veiled knowledge really is. [In the last few years, they have preferred to be called the Nation of Gods and Earths. The men are referred to as "gods" and the women are referred to as "earths"] - *We have been informed recently by a member that Allah "The Father" , Clarence 13X, said that after 1967 they would no longer be known as the 5% Nation of Islam, but as Allah's Nation of Gods and Earths.*

2. How did this message spread?

This message was delivered as a street rap that mesmerized New York City youth. They won converts by the hundreds. Today the group numbers in the tens of thousands in NYC alone. This message was also well-timed, as the 1960's were obviously a time of great struggle for blacks in America. This was a message [very similar to the black supremacist doctrines of the NOI] that made black youths feel superior in a world where they were viewed as wholly inferior.

3. How popular is it?

This sect is popular among many African-American male youth, especially in poor, urban areas. However, this thinking is also embraced by well off individuals. Its popularity is helped along by many R&B/Hip-Hop artists. Erykah Badu, Nas, Common, Wu-Tang, Busta Rhymes, and countless others have their lyric laced with 5% doctrine. In addition to using these beliefs in their music some rap artists like Rakim, Big Daddy Kane and Lakim Shabazz have used the 5% flag on their album covers. Their numbers are believed to be in the hundreds of thousands, however they personally claim many more members. The concentration of Five Percenters is believed to be the highest on the East Coast, not coincidentally to be the location of the birth of rap and hip hop music. The major cities that boast the largest African-American populations can be known to have a significant number of Five Percent adherents. These cities include: New York, New Jersey, New Have, Washington D.C., Chicago, Detroit, Philadelphia, Cleveland, Baltimore and Atlanta (to name a few). This belief system has been embraced by some internationally as well.

4. What are the requirements for membership?

The requirements of "official" membership in the Five Percent are unclear. They do not have organized affiliation. A Five

Percenter will frequently say that they simply came into knowledge of self, or better yet, the "fact" that the "Asiatic Black Man" is God... It is more a way of life and they would shun any reference to them being a "religion". They refer to "knowledging 120" (120 refers to their lessons which are virtually identical to the Supreme Wisdom originated by Elijah Muhammad and W.D. Fard). This question of whether they have "knowledged" (mastered/understood) these lessons appears to be rather important because often you will hear them say: "I knowledged 120 in [plug year in here]". In many dialogues or "builds" among themselves, disagreements are usually met with challenges to a member's knowledge of 120.

Suffice it to say that this step of absorbing the lessons likely separates the babies from the seasoned, and at the same time can expose a perpetrator. As indicated on a section of their homepage, they appear to really keep up with the rap artists level of commitment to their teachings, regardless of whether or not they pepper their lyrics with their lingo.

There are also, Parliaments and Schools that the members attend, which are meeting places where lessons are distributed and members can listen to speakers and meet others.

Additionally, there is an emphasis on knowing the history of the Five Percent, having an understanding of the Nation's flag, and being aware of Clarence 13X's legacy. Another lesson, *Teachings for the Civilized*, is also of some interest. There is an underground newspaper that is offered by subscription only. We have also discovered a newsletter called, "The Black 7." The lessons and paper have a wide circulation in prisons, where the Five Percent have mounted a significant outreach campaign. Underground book are circulated as well. Common terminology that originated with the Five Percent: "Break it down", "droppin' science", "sup G [God]?", "word", "peace", "word is bond", and "represent".

Five Percent Basic Beliefs (from NGE website via blackapologetics.com)*

1. *That black people are the original people of the planet earth.*

2. *That black people are the fathers and mothers of civilization.*

3. *That the science of Supreme Mathematics is the key to understanding man's relationship to the universe.*

4. *Islam is a natural way of life, not a religion.*

5. *That education should be fashioned to enable us to be self-sufficient as a people.*

6. *That each one should teach one according to their knowledge.*

7. *That the blackman is god and his proper name is ALLAH. Arm, Leg, Leg, Arm, Head.*

8. *That our children are our link to the future and they must be nurtured, respected, loved, protected and educated.*

9. *That the unified black family is the vital building block of the nation*

10. *That black people are the original people of the planet earth.* Adam and Eve were God's first creation and the bible does not reveal what the pigmentation of their skin was. [Genesis 2] Galatians 3:28 states: *There is neither Jew nor Greek, slave nor free, male nor female, for you are all one in Christ Jesus.* Acts 17:26 says *"from one man he made every nation of men, that they should inhabit the whole earth; and he determined the times set for them and the exact places where they should live."* Although the Bible is silent on the issue of Adam and Eve's ethnicity, race does not mean that we should not study the rich African culture/contributions that are woven into its history. However, it does mean that we should not use race to elevate ourselves over

any other race. No matter how the world feels about it, there is ultimately one race - the human race.

11. **That black people are the fathers and mothers of civilization** (See number 1).

12. **That the science of Supreme Mathematics is the key to understanding man's relationship to the universe.** God's Word, which is revealed through the Holy Bible is the key to understanding man's relationship to the universe (John 3:16; Ephesians 2:10). The bible warns us against making the principles of the world superior to Christ. Colossians 2:8 says, "See to it that no one takes you captive through hollow and deceptive philosophy, which depends on human tradition and the basic principles of this world rather than on Christ."

13. **Islam is a natural way of life, not a religion.** Islam is indeed a religion. It has the criteria of all other world religions in that there are works involved in "salvation" or "right standing" with god or gods.

14. **The five pillars of Islam must be considered:** (1) The Shahada is the Islamic proclamation that "There is no true God except Allah and Muhammad is the Messenger of Allah." (2) The daily ritual prayers (Salat) which are usually done 5 times daily between sunrise and sunset. (3) Fasting (Saum) is fasting which there is no drinking, eating, use of nicotine or sexual relations during the daylight hours for the entire month of Ramadan. (4) Alms-giving (Zakat) is a sort of tithe that Muslims are encouraged to partake in. (5) Pilgrimage (Hajj) is the pilgrimage to Mecca. If Muslims are financially able they are encouraged to take this trip.

Of course when a Five Percenter uses the term "Islam" it can certainly mean a form of Islam that they find acceptable. Black Muslims who follow the teachings of Elijah

Muhammad or both the teachings of Elijah Muhammad and Louis Farrakhan will most likely reject or ignore some of the five pillars of Orthodox Islam. In any case there is no indication that Islam is a natural way of life and not a religion. There is sufficient evidence to reveal Islam as a world religion. There are a multitude of non-Christian authors who will agree with this assessment. According to Muslim's own writings, a non-Muslim is considered an "infidel" and worthy of death. Killing another person for not ascribing to your worldview doesn't sound like a "natural way of life" it sounds like an oppressive belief system that promotes savagery and murder.

15. *That education should be fashioned to enable us to be self-sufficient as a people.* This appears to be a harmless statement, but the concern here is the *kind* of education that is being promoted. Educating blacks that they are a superior race or that the black man is god is absurd. We agree that a detailed examination of one's heritage is necessary, as well as the generations coming after us, but this standard applies to all ethnicities. Furthermore, when that examination utilizes twisted/liberal scholarship that yields questionable conclusions, then this tenet has to be flatly rejected.

16. *That each one should teach one according to their knowledge.* Not all knowledge is good knowledge. This statement hints at a premise that assumes everyone's knowledge is equally legitimate. This is not true. We have to be able to rationally and logically examine "knowledge" before we accept any teaching.

17. *That the black man is god and his proper name is ALLAH (Arm, Leg, Leg, Arm, Head).* What is amazing about this unverified assertion and adoption of this acronym is that it is accepted as fact. A direct quote from a "god" taken from

this website says: "We **know** that the Original Man (Black, Brown, Red and Yellow) is God, the Supreme Being, Allah. We do not subscribe to a mystery (unknown) God in heaven, supernatural or superhuman powers." We do not believe that this quote misrepresents what a member of the Nation of Gods and Earths believes. We see this statement over and over again in dialogue and on various websites. We find it hard to believe that there is a denial that the above is indeed a belief and not fact. Any rational thinking person can conclude that believing in the Nation of Gods and Earths ideology certainly takes a degree of faith.

The statement that there is no God is not a logical position to hold since to know there is no God means the person would have to know ALL things to know there is no God. Since one cannot know all things (if he did, he would be God [of course the 5% ARE claiming to be god, but not God in the sense that they are omnipresent and omnipotent]), then one cannot logically say there is no God.

Stating that the "black man is god" can be categorized as taking the Lord's Name in vain, which we are commanded not to do (Exodus 20:7). However, by their own admission, the "god" that the black man is referring to is not the Almighty Jehovah God of the Bible.

Many Five Percenters deny God's existence altogether and refer to Him as a "spook." We can only preclude that this is an atheist/humanist position that is masked by rhetoric that elevates the black man to a "god-like" position. In any case, the black man certainly is not taking credit for creating the world and all that is in it. Therefore, the "god" that they refer to themselves as is not God as Christians would define Him.

18. *That our children are our link to the future and they must be nurtured, respected, loved, protected and educated.*
19. *That the unified black family is the vital building block of the nation.*

Notes

THE
WATCHTOWER

JEHOVAH'S WITNESS

"THE WATCHTOWER"

Charles Taze Russell founded the Watchtower Tract Society in the 1870's. The members of the Watchtower Society later became known as Jehovah's Witnesses in 1931. Russell was moved to begin the Society as a result of his disenfranchisement with the Christian church.

DOCTRINE

Jehovah's Witnesses believe that Jesus Christ was God's first creation. He is believed to be the Word of God in a pre-human state—a means of approaching God in prayer and that His death occurred upon a torture stake as opposed to a cross. It is also believed that Jesus was the archangel Michael.

EVANGELIZING JEHOVAH'S WITNESSES

In approaching a brother or sister of the Jehovah's Witnesses one must first be grounded soundly in his or her own beliefs. Witnesses have proof texts for all of their erroneous doctrines. The Watchtower is a works based religious system in which members strive to be accounted worthy to escape God's judgment and be one of the 144,000. In order to counter this, a believer sharing his faith must be well-grounded in what salvation is and how it is obtained. The Christian Apologist should share verses like Ephesians 2:8-9 and stress how salvation is not earned by gaining a substantial number of points, but through accepting the sacrifice of Jesus Christ.

"For by grace are ye saved through faith; and that not of yourselves: it is the gift of God: Not of works, lest any man should boast."

~ Ephesians 2:8-9

The Deity of Jesus Christ is the most debated doctrine concerning Jesus' identity. Who was Jesus Christ? Is Jesus Christ God? The main focus of this information will be demonstrating Biblically that Jesus Christ is God.

"Therefore I said to you that you will die in your sins; for unless you believe that I am He, you will die in your sins."

~ John 8:24 NASB

The Deity of Jesus Christ & Misunderstandings

Some people misunderstand the doctrine of Jesus Christ being by nature God. Some people say: "Your doctrine is of the devil and is confusing...Jesus is not God because the Father alone is God...Jesus cannot be God because Jesus is the Son of God." Those who say the doctrine of Jesus Christ being God is of the devil have not come to understand what the Scriptures teach in context and they have been blinded by the ways of the world (Colossians 2:1-9). For those who have not come to know Jesus Christ personally and do not have the Holy Spirit to give them spiritual understanding state this doctrine is confusing, and honestly without the Holy Spirit this doctrine is confusing (1 Corinthians 2:14-16). Those who say Jesus is not God because the Father alone is God misunderstand what Christians believe concerning the nature of Jesus. Jesus Christ is a distinct personage from the Father, He came to reveal the heart of the Father, and is by nature and identity God from eternity (John 1:1-18; Phil. 2:5-11). Jesus Christ is the Son of God but that does not mean that He is not by nature and identity God. The title, *"the Son of God"*, in regards to Jesus Christ refers to His equality with God (the Father), which is a way of expressing His Deity in the flesh (John 5:18-23). Jesus being the Son of God shows He is a distinct personage from the Father and at the same time by identity God in the flesh. Jesus is also called the *"Son of Man"* which identifies Him as both Messiah and Lord (Matthew 12:8), yet no one will say that Jesus was not man in the flesh, in the likeness of mankind.

What Does the Bible Teach About the Deity of Jesus Christ?

The Bible teaches that there is one God to be served and all other so called gods are not genuine or true (Isa. 43:10; Gal. 4:8). The Bible teaches that Jesus Christ is God in the flesh sent from the Father to redeem mankind from their sins (John 1:1, 14, 3:16; Matt. 1:21-23). Those who say the Bible does not teach the Deity of Jesus Christ have come to wrong conclusions, thus misunderstanding the context and overall emphasis of who God is.

What Do Other Religious Groups Believe About the Deity of Jesus Christ?

Jehovah's Witnesses deny the Deity of Jesus Christ by teaching that He is the first of God's creation, also called Michael the archangel. Jehovah's Witnesses have been deceived with another Jesus through the Watchtower Bible and Tract Society's false teachings. Mormons don't believe in only one God, but in many Gods, and they believe Jesus became a God thus rejecting His eternal Deity. There are many sincere Mormons who believe in Jesus but they do not have the Jesus of the Bible. Islam rejects the Deity of Jesus Christ and Him being the Son of God. Muslims do believe in Jesus as being a prophet of God but they have a wrong Biblical view of who He is and what He came to do. The dividing line of any religious group is on the Deity of Jesus Christ. There were many who opposed the true identity of Jesus Christ among the early Church and there have been many throughout history (Matt 7:15, 21-23, Acts 20:23-31, 2 Cor. 11:4, 13-15, Col. 2:1-9, 1 Tim. 4:1-3, 2 Tim. 4:2-5).

Knowing the Jesus of the Bible

The Bible teaches eternity is at stake with or without knowing Jesus personally. If you do not know the Jesus of the Bible you are not saved, but there is hope. God's desire is for anyone to be saved and come to know Jesus Christ personally (2 Pet. 3:9). Scriptures on knowing Jesus Christ personally are: *Matthew 5:1-7:29, Matthew 10:22-32, Matthew 16:24-26, John 1:1-18, John 3:14-18, John 5:24, John 8:24, John 14:1-6, John 16:7-15, John 20:24-31, Romans 1:16-17, Romans 3:21-31, Romans 4:1-6, Romans 5:1-10, Romans 10:9-13, 1 John 1:1-10, 1 John 5:10-13 & 20.*

"[1.] For I want you to know how great a struggle I have on your behalf and for those who are at Laodicea, and for all those who have not personally seen my face, [2.] that their hearts may be encouraged, having been knit together in love, and attaining to all the wealth that comes from the full assurance of understanding, resulting in a true knowledge of God's mystery, that is, Christ Himself, [3.] in whom are hidden all the treasures of wisdom and knowledge. [4.] I say this so that no one will delude you with persuasive argument. [5.] For even though I am absent in body, nevertheless I am with you in spirit, rejoicing to see your good discipline and the stability of your faith in Christ. [6.] Therefore as you have received Christ Jesus the Lord, so walk in Him, [7.] having been firmly rooted and now being built up in Him and established in your faith, just as you were instructed, and overflowing with gratitude. [8.] See to it that no one takes you captive through philosophy and empty deception, according to the tradition of men, according to the elementary principles of the world, rather than according to Christ [9.] For in Him all the fullness of Deity dwells in bodily form"

~ **Colossians 2:1-9 NASB**

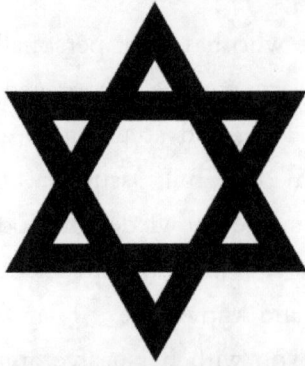

JUDAISM

"THE DOCTRINE OF THE JEWS"

According to the Biblical text, Judaism originates from the Abrahamic era. Christianity and Islam are believed to originate as descendants of Judaism. The Bible confirms Christianity as a beneficiary of Judaism, however, the Bible makes no reference of Islam.

Judaism originated in the Middle East. Some schools of thought assert that Judaism was founded by Moses, however, Judaism can be traced all the way back to Abraham. According to the Jewish faith, there is only one God, and through God's covenant with the Jews, they are His chosen people. To honor God for His goodness, Jews attempt to keep God's laws and try to embody holiness within every aspect of their lives. The most fundamental and important religious document within Judaism is the Torah. Religious leaders are called Rabbis. Jews worship in Synagogues.

DOCTRINE

Jews believe that there is only one God, who is not only the creator of all that exist, but He is also able to have a personal relationship with every individual. The Jewish relationship with God is a covenant based relationship, very similar to a husband and wife. As a result of God's goodness and chastisement throughout the ages, Jews attempt to obey God's commandments in pursuit of holiness. Jews believe that God appointed the Jews to be his chosen people in order to be a beacon of holiness and morality to the world.

Judaism is a faith of good works by obedience to all of God's laws. Jews believe people should be judged not so much by the intellectual content of their beliefs, but by the way they live their faith - by how much they contribute to the overall holiness of the world. According to Judaism, God is not a triune being (unlike the Christian view of the Trinity). God is superior to everything. God is a spirit and has no physical body. God is omnipresent, being everywhere, all the time. God is omnipotent because He can do anything. God is beyond time and has always existed. God does not change. God punishes those that commit evil and rewards those that do well. God is personal, accessible, and is interested in every aspect of each individual's life.

JESUS ACCORDING TO JUDAISM

Jesus is not the Messiah according to Jewish standards because He did not fulfill their conditions. Jews do not accept Jesus as the Messiah because they assert that He did not fulfill the Messianic prophecies or embody the personal qualifications of the Messiah, among several other criteria. According to Judaism, no one has fulfilled the Messianic prophecies of this Jewish King, therefore, Jews still wait for the coming of the Messiah.

Many Jews assume that the life of Jesus described in the Gospels are from four different contradictory angles. Therefore, Jews should be encouraged to read the New Testament Scriptures for themselves. Jews that sincerely read each of the gospels in particular would likely comprehend that the writers merely wrote from their personal perspectives. For example, one understandably grasps Matthew's approach in his attempt to prove that all the prophecies relating to the Messiah were manifested in Jesus.

The Jewish Messiah

The *mashiach* will be a great political leader descended directly from the bloodline of King David (Jeremiah 23:5). The mashiach is often referred to as "mashiach ben David" (mashiach, son of David). He will be well-versed in Jewish law, and observant of its commandments (Isaiah 11:2-5). He will be a charismatic leader, inspiring others to follow his example. He will be a great military leader, who will win battles for Israel. He will be a great judge, who makes righteous decisions (Jeremiah 33:15). But above all, he will be a human being, not a god, demi-god or other supernatural being.[57]

Credentials of the Messiah According to Judaism

1. When the Messiah reigns as King of Israel, the Jewish people will be ingathered from the 2,000 year exile, and will return to Israel (Deut. 30:3; Isa. 11:11-12; Jer. 30:3; 32:37; Ez. 11:17, 36:24).
2. The Temple in Israel will be rebuilt (Isa. 2:2-3, 56:6-7, 60:7, 66:20; Ez. 37:26-27; Malachi 3:4; Zech. 14:20-21).
3. There will be worldwide peace, universal disarmament and completely end war (Micah 4:1-4; Hos. 2:20; Isa. 2:1-4, 60:18).
4. The Messiah will reign as King at a time when all the Jewish people embrace the Torah and observe all of God's

commandments (Ez. 37:24; Deut. 30:8, 10; Jer. 31:32; Ez. 11:19-20, 36:26-27).

5. The Messiah will rule at a time when all the people of the world come to knowledge and serve the one true God of Abraham, Isaac and Jacob (Zech. 3:9, 8:23, 14:9, 16; Isa. 45:23, 66:23; Jer. 31:33; Ez. 38:23; Ps. 86:9; Zeph. 3:9).

6. The Messiah will come from the Tribe of Judah and be a direct descendant of king David and king Solomon (Gen. 49:10; 2 Sam. 7:12-14; 1 Chr. 22:9-10).

According to Matthew 1:18-20, Jesus was not biologically conceived by an earthly father because His conception was of the Holy Ghost. Many orthodox-Jews affirm that pedigree is strictly determined through the lineage of the father (Num. 1:1-18). For that reason, they denounce Jesus as descendant of King David. However, when the father is absent the conclusion of book of Leviticus affirms that pedigree can be identified through the mother (Lev. 24:10-11). Within this text, the name of the father is not mentioned. All that was mentioned was his nationality. However, the pedigree of the mother is mentioned in the absent father's place.

There are several other messianic interpretations for the Messiah, but none of these Jewish qualifications of the Messiah are contextually backed by Old Testament Scriptures. Many orthodox-Jews will profess that the Messiah will come within these credential, however, Old Testament Scriptures do not specify that the Messiah was determined to come within the manner of their interpretations.

Some Jews even believe that Jesus realized He actually did not meet the criteria of the messiah when He cried aloud, "My God. My God. Why have you forsaken me? (Matthew 27:46)" They have adopted the notion that Jesus was inadvertently expressing the recognition of His failure to fulfill the messianic prophecies. Many orthodox-Jews assert that missionary Christians profess that Jesus will accomplish them when He returns in the future. They believe that the doctrine of the second coming is an admission that Jesus did not fulfill the messianic criteria. For that reason, they denounce Him as the Messiah.

COMMON JEWISH CUSTOMS

The Sabbath is Commanded by God

Every week religious Jews observe the Sabbath, the Jewish holy day, and keep its laws and customs. The Sabbath begins at nightfall on Friday and lasts until nightfall on Saturday. In practical terms the Sabbath starts a few minutes before sunset on Friday and runs until an hour after sunset on Saturday, so it lasts about 25 hours.

God commanded the Jewish People to observe the Sabbath and keep it holy as the fourth of the Ten Commandments. The idea of a day of rest comes from the Bible story of the Creation: God rested from creating the universe on the seventh day of that first week, so Jews rest from work on the Sabbath. Jews often call the day Shabbat, which is Hebrew for Sabbath, and which comes from the Hebrew word for rest. The Sabbath is part of the deal between God and the Jewish People, so celebrating it is a reminder of the Covenant and an occasion to rejoice in God's kept promises.

The Kippah/Yarmulke

Clothing worn by Jews usually varies according to which denomination of Judaism they adhere to. Orthodox Jewish men always cover their heads by wearing a skullcap known in Hebrew as a kippah or in Yiddish as a yarmulke. Liberal or Reform Jews see the covering of the head as optional. Most Jews will cover their heads when praying, attending the synagogue or at a religious event or festival. Wearing a skullcap is seen as a sign of devoutness. Women also cover their heads by wearing a scarf or a hat. The most common reason (for covering the head) is a sign of respect and fear of God. It is also felt that this separates God and human, by wearing a hat you are recognizing that God is above all mankind.

SACRED TEXT

What is the Torah?

The Torah is the first part of the Jewish bible. It is the central and most important document of Judaism and has been used by Jews through the ages. Torah refers to the five books of Moses which are known in Hebrew as Chameesha Choomshey Torah. These are: Bresheit (Genesis), Shemot (Exodus), Vayicra (Leviticus), Bamidbar (Numbers), and Devarim (Deuteronomy).

Jews believe that God dictated the Torah to Moses on Mount Sinai 50 days after their exodus from Egyptian slavery. They believe that the Torah shows how God wants Jews to live. It contains 613 commandments and Jews refer to the ten best known of these as the ten 10 statements. The Torah is written in Hebrew, the oldest of Jewish languages. It is also known as Torat Moshe, the Law of Moses. The Torah is the first section or first five books of the Jewish bible. However, Tanach is more commonly used to describe the whole of Jewish scriptures. This is an acronym made up from the first letter of the words Torah, Nevi im (prophets), and Ketuvim (writings).

Similarly, the term Torah is sometimes used in a more general sense to incorporate Judaism's written and oral law. This definition encompasses Jewish scripture in its entirety including all authoritative Jewish religious teachings throughout history. The word Torah has various meanings in English., which include teaching, instruction and law. For Jews the Torah means all of these.

How is the Torah Used?

The Torah scrolls are taken out from the Ark (*Aron ha kodesh*) and portions read in the synagogue three times each week. On Mondays and Thursdays small sections are read. The main reading is on the morning of *Shabbat* (Sabbath). Over the course of the year the whole scroll is read in sequence. This begins from the end of *Sukkot* which is an autumn festival. The special portions for the readings are called *parshioth* and are usually three to five chapters in length. The reader has to be very skilled to read from the scroll because the letters are written without corresponding vowels. They have to know the portion very well to avoid making mistakes. The reading is conducted using an ancient tune and is sung rather than spoken.

The scrolls are not directly touched when unfurled on the *Bimah* (raised platform in middle of the synagogue). A pointer or *Yad* (hand) is used instead. This is in the shape of a hand with an outstretched finger. The reading or chanting is performed by a person who has been trained in this task. However it may be carried out by the rabbi. It is a very great honour for a congregant to be asked to attend at a reading during a synagogue service. This is called having an *Aliyah* which is Hebrew for *going up*. The weekly portion or *Sedrah* is followed by the recitation of part of another of the Jewish holy writings.

Conclusion

Jesus Christ is the fulfillment of the Biblical prophecies of the Messiah. The Jews disqualify Jesus solely based on their interpretation of Scripture and stipulations for a Messiah, but we know that God does things in His own timing and in His own way (Isa. 55:8; Ps. 92:5). One of the most accurate descriptions of Jesus is found within Isaiah 53:3-7, "He (Jesus) is despised and rejected by men. He was a man of sorrows, acquainted with grief, and we hid as it were *our* faces from him. He was despised, and we did not esteemed. 4. Surely, he has lifted our griefs, and carried our sorrows. Yet, we considered him plague, smitten, and afflicted by God. 5. But, he *was* wounded for our transgressions. He was bruised on account of our iniquities. The chastisement of our peace *was* upon him, and with his stripes, we are healed. 6. Like sheep, we have all gone astray. Each one of us have gone our own way, and the LORD has laid on him the iniquity of us all. 7. He was oppressed, and he was afflicted, yet he did not open his mouth. He was brought as a lamb to the slaughter, and as a sheep before her shearers is dumb, but he still did not open his mouth."

These words from Isaiah are a perfect reflection of the sacrifice Jesus paid on the Cross for our sins. When witnessing to Jews, don't assume that they are well versed in the scriptures. Inviting Jewish associates to church is not a substitute for personally sharing your faith. If there are questions you are unable to answer, tell them you would like the opportunity to research it for them. Hopefully, this will give you further witnessing opportunities. You may not be able to answer all of their questions, but share the Gospel of Jesus Christ with boldness and compassion.

MORMONISM

"THE CHURCH OF LATTER DAY SAINTS"

The Church of Latter Day Saints was founded by Joseph Smith in 1830.[58] As legend would have it, Smith was approached by an angel named Moroni that gave him special equipment for excavating a hidden treasure, which happened to be a set of Golden Plates.[59] These plates contained what is currently called the Book of Mormon.[60] The main premise behind Mormon theology is that some of the Israelites got on a boat and traveled to America later becoming the Indians or Native Americans in existence today.[61]

Mormons deny the deity of Christ and relegate Him to a position of a mere man.[62] Mormons also believe that Christ had children. Further adding insult to injury is the fact that Mormons accept the Bible as the Word of God only to the extent that it is "interpreted correctly."[63]

Members of the Mormon faith are well-versed in their belief

system. Males within Mormonism are required to be missionaries often traveling to different countries to ministries on behalf of the Mormon faith.[64] Due to these efforts many have been baptized into the Mormon Church. A Bible-believing Christian must first be well-versed in what they personally believe before addressing a Mormon. The identity of Christ should be addressed along with the substance of the Book of Mormon. Most Mormon missionaries are very open in terms of what they believe and will freely disclose these beliefs when asked. John 10:16 and the concept of other sheep is often quoted and used by Mormons. Study this verse fully to gain understanding into what Christ was speaking about and share this information lovingly with a Mormon brother or sister. Ultimately, the Christian Apologist should challenge a brother or sister within Mormonism to an honest study of the Bible.

"And other sheep I have, which are not of this fold: them also I must bring, and they shall hear my voice; and there shall be one fold, and one shepherd."

~ John 10:16

"Study to show thyself approved unto God, a workman that needeth not to be ashamed, rightly dividing the word of truth."

~ 2 Timothy 2:15

Reasons We Believe Mormonism is False and Not of God

1. Mormonism is polytheistic.[65]
2. Mormonism teaches that God was once a man who became a God. But the Bible teaches God has always been God and was not once a man who became a God (Psalms 90:2).[66]
3. Mormonism teaches that Jesus is the spirit brother of Lucifer. But the Bible teaches Jesus is not the brother of

Lucifer but the very One who created him (John 1:3; Colossians 1:16-17).

4. Mormonism teaches that the blood of Jesus does not atone for all sins, but certain sins you must atone for yourself.[67] But the Bible teaches the blood of Jesus Christ atones for all sins and cleanses us from all unrighteousness (1 John 1:7, 9).

5. Mormonism teaches that men can become Gods.[68] God alone is God and the Bible is clear that no one can become a God (Isaiah 43:10).

6. Mormonism teaches that salvation is found only in the Mormon Church.[69] However the Bible teaches that salvation is not found in the Mormon Church but in being born again through faith in Jesus Christ (John 3:3-18, 14:6; 1 John 5:10-13).

Mormon doctrine that sounds Biblical

1. Mormons say they believe in Jesus but the Jesus they serve is not the Biblical Jesus: The Jesus of the Mormon Church is the brother of Lucifer. Jesus is a spirit child of God the Father and a heavenly mother by physical union (sex). Jesus was born a child and through obedience to the Laws became a God, therefore Jesus has not always been God. Jesus' shed blood on the cross does not atone for all sins, but there are certain sins that the blood of Jesus does not atone for. Jesus after He was crucified and raised to life married three women and had offspring.

2. Mormons say they believe in God the Father but He is not the same One from the Bible: Mormons believe that God the Father was once a man who became a God. Mormons believe that God the Father had a father, and his father

had a father, an endless progression of Gods.[70] That means God has not always been God, but the Father was at one time not God by nature.

3. Mormons say they believe in the Trinity, but their definition is different. The Mormon Church teaches that the Father, Jesus, and the Holy Spirit (Trinity) are three different Gods.[71] Mormons believe the Trinity is one in purpose not in nature.

4. Mormons say they are the only true Church. The Mormon Church teaches that they are the only true Church and that all others are the Church of the devil. They may not say this to you, but they do teach this.

5. Mormons say they believe in the Bible. The Mormon Church teaches that there are 4 holy books. These books are: the Book of Mormon, the Pearl of Great Price, Doctrines and Covenants, and the Bible.[72] The Bible in the Mormon Church is least looked upon for doctrine and theology. Mormons are taught that the Bible is correct as long as it goes with their theology. If the Bible contradicts what the other 3 books say or their theology, than the Bible is wrong according to the Mormon Church.[73]

NEW AGE

"ALL IS GOD"

"For God doth know that in the day ye eat thereof, then your eyes shall be opened, and ye shall be as gods, knowing good and evil."

~ **Genesis 3:5**

"[The new age movement is] the renewal of ancient occultism, but with organization. Many of the new age groups stress movement away from the God of the bible to the god within." ~ **Walter Martin**

"When a man ceases to believe in God, he does not believe in nothing, he believes in anything." ~ **G.K. Chesterton**

"When I use a word... it means just what I choose it to mean—neither more nor less." ~ **Quote from *Humpty Dumpty* in Lewis Carrol's *Alice Through the Looking Glass***

HISTORICAL BACKGROUND

The New Age Movement (NAM), also known as Spiritualism, is a spin-off of many of the Eastern religions such as Hinduism and Buddhism. These movements in their various forms stress the principle that all is one and carries the misconception begun by Satan in the Garden of Eden to further error (Genesis 3:4-6). The influence of the New Age Movement permeates society with expressions of Mother Earth, Father Time, movies (e.g. Star Wars), music, and even the current homosexual movement. The basis of this movement is that man is god and has the ability to manipulate his environment to suit his needs. Entities, such as God, do no more than hinder the overall actualization of this god-like status and, therefore, are not followed. Some of the basic beliefs of New Age proponents include: God is impersonal, man is divine, salvation is correct thought and practice, and miracles come from the mind of man (i.e., scientific innovation, resolving a personal problem one was having).

Ye are of your father the devil, and the lusts of your father ye will do. He was a murderer from the beginning, and abode not in the truth, because there is no truth in him. When he speaketh a lie, he speaketh of his own: for he is a liar, and the father of it. ~ **John 8:44**

In whom the god of this world hath blinded the minds of them which believe not, lest the light of the glorious gospel of Christ, who is the image of God, should shine unto them. ~ **2 Corinthians 4:4**

Some very famous and influential people you probably didn't know endorsed or are currently adherents of the New Age agenda:

- Eckhart Tolle
- Oprah Winfrey

- Shirley MacLaine
- Deepak Chopra
- Montel Williams
- Dr. Wayne Dyer
- Rhonda Byrne (author of "The Secret")

The list goes on and on, making it imperative that Christians also be careful regarding who they follow and admire. The writer of First John said, "Beloved, believe not every spirit, but try the spirits whether they are of God: because many false prophets are gone out into the world" (1 John 4:1).

Biblical Responses to the New Age Movement

1. God is personal. If God were impersonal, then the following qualities could not be His.
   a. God speaks and has a self-given name: "I AM" (Exodus 3:14).
   b. God is long suffering, (Psalm 86:15; 2 Peter 3:15).
   c. God is forgiving (Daniel 9:9; Ephesians 1:7; Psalm 86:5).
   d. God hates sin (Psalm 5:5-6; Habakkuk 1:13).
2. Man is not divine, but a sinner (Romans 3:23).
   a. He is deceitful and desperately sick (Jer. 17:9).
   b. He is full of evil (Mark 7:21-23).
   c. He loves darkness rather than light (John 3:19).
   d. He is unrighteous, does not understand, and does not seek for God (Rom. 3:10-12).
   e. He is helpless and ungodly (Rom. 5:6).
   f. He is dead in his trespasses and sins (Eph. 2:1).
   g. He is by nature a child of wrath (Eph. 2:3).
   h. He cannot understand spiritual things (1 Cor. 2:14).

3. Salvation is not correct thought, but deliverance from the consequence of our sin (Romans 6:23; Ephesians 2:8-9).

    a. Salvation is God's deliverance from damnation (Eph. 2:8-9; Rom. 1:18; 2:5; 5:9).

    b. This salvation is found in no one but Jesus alone (Acts 4:12).

4. Miracles are from God not from the mind of man (Matthew 8:1-4; Mark 6:30-44; Luke 17:12-19; John 2:1-11).

    a. Miracles imply an action by someone that is greater than ourselves. If God is impersonal, miracles cannot occur. But they do occur today as well as in Bible times and are not simply proper thoughts or understanding.

5. Christ means "anointed. Jesus was the Christ, the anointed one." It does not mean a consciousness or quality of people. Jesus was the Christ, the Messiah, and the Deliverer from sin.

    a. Jesus is the Christ (Matt. 16:16, 20; Luke 9:20).

    b. *"Was it not necessary for the Christ to suffer these things and to enter into His glory"* (Luke 24:26).

    c. *"Thus it is written, that the Christ should suffer and rise again from the dead the third day"* (Luke 24:46).

    d. *"...we have found the Messiah (which translated means Christ)"* (John 1:41).

    e. *"He [David] looked ahead and spoke of the resurrection of the Christ..."* (Acts 2:31).

    f. *"...God has made Him both Lord and Christ this Jesus whom you crucified"* (Acts 2:36).

    g. *"For while we were still helpless, at the right time Christ died for the ungodly"* (Rom. 5:6).

    h. *"Therefore we have been buried with Him through baptism into death, in order that as Christ was raised from the dead through*

> *the glory of the Father, so we too might walk in newness of life"* (Rom. 6:4).

    i.   Christ is crucified (1 Cor. 1:23).

    j.   You sin against Christ (1 Cor. 8:12).

    k.   The blood of Christ (1 Cor. 10:16).

6. Only the Bible has the message of Grace. Grace is the unmerited favor of God upon His people. Grace is the undeserved kindness of God. Grace is getting the blessings we do not deserve. At the death of Christ we are blessed; we are given grace; we are given eternal life and forgiveness of sins. Only Christianity has the message of free forgiveness given. Every other religious system on Earth has some form of salvation dependent totally or in part on what the adherents do. Not so with Christianity.

7. Humanity is not unlimited, but just the opposite: it is under bondage (Romans 5:12). Sin is its master and a deadly and deceitful one at that.

8. True morality is that which is revealed by God in the Bible (Exodus 20). Anything else is only an imitation, a set of ideas laid down by man that originate from the mind of sinful man.

9. The Bible opposes almost all the tenets of the New Age Movement. As Christians, we should be watchful to recognize what is false and teach what is true. We should be wary because the Edenic lie still rings strong in the hearts of the deceived -- and they want us to believe as they.

Witnessing to New Agers

1. **Ask questions**

    a.   If we are all God, then why do we act so badly?

        i.   They might say it is because we all have not come to a full realization of our true divine potentials. It is ignorance that leads to bad deeds.

ii. Then ask them how, if we are divine, our mere ignorant self could so easily override our divine goodness.

b. Why do our "realities" contradict each other?

i. They might say that they don't contradict each other. They are simply different shades of light on the same picture (or something vague like that).

ii. Then ask if truth contradicts itself. It does not. The logic is that if we are all in different forms of truth, then these different truths can't ultimately contradict each other--or they wouldn't be true.

a. The NAM says that Jesus is only one of many ways to God. But Jesus said He was the only way to God (John 14:6). They can't both be right; therefore, the NAM teaching that we can create our own truths can't be true.

2. **Don't let them take Christian words and use them out of the context of biblical meaning.**

a. New Agers recognize the tremendous influence and spotless reputation of Jesus. They want Him to be associated with their beliefs. As a result, you might find yourself facing a New Ager who uses Christian words--but with non-Christian definitions. Listen carefully, and don't let them steal what is Christian and transplant it into their system.

b. You must question the terms they use. You need to make sure that what they mean by Christian terms is the same thing that you mean by them.

3. **Listen for internal contradictions.**

   a. As mentioned above, truth does not contradict itself. You must listen to what they are saying and ask questions. Sooner or later you catch on to inconsistencies. Inconsistencies usually arise when discussing the relationship between reality and belief. For example, a New Ager might say that you can create your own reality. I might reply, "Good. Then if I believe red lights are really green, would you want to go driving with me?"

4. **Tell them that God is personal, that he loves them, and that Jesus died for sin.**

   a. The Word of God will not come back empty without accomplishing what God wishes it to (Isaiah 55:11). If you focus on Jesus, tell them the truth about sin and salvation, and use Scripture, then, at least, they will have heard the truth. Praise be to Jesus the Christ.

   b. Remember, God's word is powerful. Whether or not they accept it isn't the issue. You simply need to present the truth in an accurate and loving manner (Col. 4:5-6; 1 Tim. 1:5).

Notes

SATANISM

"THE LIGHTBEARER"

The term Satan originates from the Hebraic word, שָׂטָן Satan (saw-tawn') meaning an *opponent*, and the arch enemy of good. Satan is also known as the *adversary*, whose sole agenda is to stand against the will of God. In Greek, as mentioned by Jesus, he is addressed as Satanas (sat-an-as'), which means the *accuser*, that is, the *devil* (of Chaldean origin).

HISTORICAL BACKGROUND

Who is Satan?

Satan was created as a distinct and unique angel, however, he allowed pride to fill his heart. Satan became arrogant in his beauty, status, and decided that he wanted to assert himself above the throne of God (Ezekiel 28:12-19). John the Revelator had the privilege of seeing a vision from God regarding everything surrounding Satan's expulsion from heaven. In the beginning of John's vision, he is shown the birth of Jesus Christ, then a large red dragon. John exclaims that the tail (i.e. influence) of the dragon drew a third of the angelic host of heaven, convincing them to align themselves with his agenda. Subsequently, a war erupts in heaven between the dragon (Lucifer) and his angels, and Michael, the arch angel and his angels, but Lucifer and his forces were not strong enough to prevail (Rev. 12:1-9).

Prior to Satan's exile, Isaiah identifies Satan as Lucifer. Ezekiel describes Lucifer as having been a Cherub, and one of the highest ranking angels. Ezekiel alludes to the beauty and office of Lucifer when he states that it was Lucifer's conceit that led to his banishment. As a result of Satan's pride, God condemned and permanently removed Lucifer from his role as Cherub (Isaiah 14:12-14, also see 1 Timothy 3:6). Through Isaiah's revelation, we can clearly see that Satan's intent was to usurp authority and overthrow God. A prevalent deception circulating is that Lucifer is not Satan. Some link the identity of Lucifer to Jesus, and others say that he is a type of messianic entity. This should be of no surprise since God's word warns that Satan disguises himself as an "angel of light," in order to deceive others (2 Corinthians 11:14). However, proper exegesis of the Bible reveals that Lucifer is Satan. When the Bible refers to the fall of Lucifer, the corresponding verses of Ezekiel 28:13-17, Luke 10:18, 2 Peter 2:4, and Revelation 12:7-10, all point to Lucifer as being Satan.

Clearly Satan doesn't change his strategy because we see the same exact methods used when he came to tempt Jesus in the wilderness:

> *"Then Jesus was led by the Spirit into the wilderness to be tempted by the devil.* ² *And when He had fasted forty days and forty nights, He became hungry.* ³ *And when the tempter came to Him, he said, 'If you are the Son of God, command that*

these stones become bread.' 4. But Jesus answered and said, 'It is written, Man will not live by bread alone, but by every word that comes out of the mouth of God.' 5. Then the devil took Him up into the holy city, and set Him on a pinnacle (top corner) of the temple, 6. And said to Him, 'If you are the Son of God, then jump [from this high place]. It is written, He will give His angels charge concerning you, and in their hands they will bear you up, in case at any time you dash your foot against a stone.' 7. Jesus replied saying, 'It is written again, You will not tempt the Lord your God.' 8. Again, the devil took him up into an extremely high mountain, and showed him all the kingdoms of the world, and the glory of them. 9. He said, 'I will give you all these things, if you will fall down and worship me.' 10. Jesus replied, 'Go away, Satan. For it is written, You will worship the Lord your God, and you will only serve Him.' 11. Then the devil left him, and angels came and ministered to him" (Matthew 4:1-11).

Satan's self-appointed mission is to accuse and tempt as many people as he can, in order to turn them from God. Satan wants us to rely on our own God-given abilities, instead of putting our faith in the Almighty. Satan wants humanity to always second guess their identity and God's Word toward us. Ultimately, Satan wants all people to serve and adore him because he envies God, and he has done so from the beginning when he said in his heart: "I will ascend into heaven. I will exalt my throne above the stars of God and I will sit upon the mount of the congregation, in the sides of the north" (Isa. 14:13). He goes on to say, "I will ascend above the heights of the clouds and I will be like the most High" (Isa. 14:14). This is the true mind of Satan, and his followers merely echo his sentiments.

Because Satan is the father of lies, there exist an abundance of confusion among Satanist (John 8:43-44). Satanic philosophies are deceptively diverse and there are several different sects of Satanism. Even Satanist argue among themselves concerning whether or not Satan exist, or if they are worshipping Satan or themselves. These misperceptions are evidence that the God of the Bible is not the originator of such doctrinal beliefs (1 Cor. 14:33). It's important to note that Satan's true agenda according to the Apostle John is to steal, kill, and destroy (John 10:10).

According to Job, there was a day when the sons of God came to present themselves before the Lord, and Satan came among them. The Lord said to Satan, "Where have you been?" Satan replied, "I've been travelling the earth and walking up and down in it" (Job 1:7). Recall that the author of 1 Peter 5:8 said, "Be sober and vigilant because your adversary the devil, walks around as a roaring lion, seeking those he can devour." Satan has made his occupation as an adversary to humanity, and he "lives and breathes" our damnation.

The Church of Satan

Satanism was brought into the mainstream by Anton Szandor LaVey, after he established the Church of Satan as a faith-based organization in 1966. LaVey was born April 11, 1930. LaVey was the first high priest of the Church of Satan, a practicing occultist, and oftentimes called himself a satanic priest. He is also the author of the Satanic Bible and the founder of LaVeyan Satanism, which are philosophers who advocated "materialism" and "individualism."[74] LaVey died on October 29, 1997. In order to better understand Satanism, we must understand the mind of Satan. A portion of Isaiah's narrative gives us a glimpse into the mindset of Satan. Isaiah said, "How you were throw down from heaven, O Lucifer, son of the morning! *How* you were cut down to the ground, which did weaken the nations! 13. Because you said in your heart, 'I will ascend into heaven, I will exalt my throne above the stars of God. I will also sit on the mount of the congregation, in the sides of the north. [14.] I will ascend above the high place of the clouds and I will be like the most High'" (Isa. 14:12-14).

LaVey stated the following in a televised interview: "Well, when I was a teenager, I was interested in the occult. And the occult in those days meant you got dream books, and you got a book on fortune telling, but the closest thing to conjuring demons or that sort of thing involved standing around in a circle, where you used the protective names of Jehovah and Jesus, and all that. I tried it..., but it didn't work. So, I thought to myself, if I'm going to call up any demons. If I'm going to get any magical powers. If I'm going to get anything going my way, then I better get on the side of those guys, instead of protecting myself from them."

During LaVey's interview, he did not speak of demons allegorically. Instead, he made direct reference to siding with them in order to receive power and influence. You can't receive power and influence from something that doesn't exist. In actuality, LaVey never believed that Satan and demons were metaphorical. In fact, he believed that they were conscious entities that he could summons. During a separate interview defining Satanism, LaVey said, "The word demon does not imply evil, but simply a guiding or motivating spirit." Within this quote, LaVey refers to demons as having the ability to influence people.

In an interview on the Joe Pyne show in the 1960's, LaVey had this to say about his perception of God: "I feel God exists, but the name of God is different for many different people, and I feel that God is that force. Whatever God one chooses to pray too... In the case of Satanism, rather than pray, I feel that whatever god exist should be the god that carries a person along..." LaVey also said, "Satan is to us, a symbol, rather than an anthropomorphic being.

Although many members of the Church of Satan, who are mystically inclined, would prefer to think of Satan in a very real anthropomorphic way. Of course, we do not discourage this because we realize that to many individuals, a picture of their mentor (Satan) is very important for them to conceptualize. However, Satan symbolically is a teacher. The informer of the "whys" and the "wherefores" of the world. And in answer to those who would label us devil worshippers, or be very quick to assume us to be Satan worshippers, I must say that Satan demands a study, not worship.

The Temple of Set

Conversely, a few followers of LaVey eventually branched off to start their own churches. Individuals like Kenneth Anger deceived many people into thinking they were worshipping the supposed "light god," rather than Satan. Eventually, Anger "confessed" that Lucifer, whom he worships, had always been the historical "Satan." Furthermore, Lieutenant Colonel Michael Aquino of the United States Army joined the Church of Satan while he was an Intelligence Officer in the U.S. Army and became a leader in LaVey's church. Aquino also branched off from LaVey to start the "Temple of Set." Aquino also appeared on the Oprah Winfrey show in 1988. The Temple of Set was later joined by Anton LaVey's daughter Zeena LaVey. The Temple of Set proclaims that "Set" is simply another name for Satan, and that he is a real entity. "We are not servants of some God," declared Aquino, "we are our own gods!"

Luciferian Philosophy

There are two primary types of the Luciferian philosophy. The first type is the worship or reverence of Lucifer as a deity. Such a religion attempts to emphasize what they consider "positive" aspects of Lucifer. Another type of Luciferian philosophy is nontheistic and views Lucifer as nothing more than a symbol of mankind's quest for wisdom and enlightenment. The name "Lucifer" comes from a translation of Isaiah 14:12. The term Lucifer comes from the Hebrew word **הֵילֵל,** heylel (*hay-lale'*) *meaning* the *morning star.*

The declaration of the Luciferian doctrine asserts that Lucifer is the "light bearer" and the true God, who brings true spiritual enlightenment to humanity through intellectual knowledge. According to the Luciferian philosophy, Lucifer "liberated" Adam and Eve, who were being held as prisoners in the Garden of God. As a fallen angel, Satan successfully encourages Adam and Eve to rebel against God's commandments. Satan has cleverly deceived the general populous into believing that disobeying God by eating of the tree of the knowledge of good and evil was an act of mercy to enlighten them from the ignorance that God used to hold them captive. As a result, man was set free from the Garden because Lucifer had given man the "gift of intellect." This alternative form of New Age philosophy teaches that through intellect, mankind will excel and create for themselves a perfect world system.

If this were possible for mankind to achieve without the governing aid of God, then such a feat would have been accomplished by now. Through knowledge, mankind would have liberated themselves long ago. However, Jesus said, "I am the vine, you *are* the branches. He that abides in me, and I in him, the same brings forth much fruit, because without me you can do nothing" (John 15:5).

Isaiah 14 and Ezekiel 28 teach that Satan was created as one of the highest ranking angels. He was also one of the most beautiful angels. However, his pride and desire to usurp God's throne resulted in him being cast out of heaven. Subsequently, he was later identified as "Satan" (meaning "adversary"). John said, "...for the accuser of our brethren is cast down, which accused them before our God day and night" (Rev. 12:10). John affirms the accusatorial character of Satan in Job 1:9-11.

The Satanic Temple

The Satanic Temple is a perfect example of a Satanic group that rejects the idea of Lucifer being a personal entity. The stated mission of "The Satanic Temple is to encourage benevolence and empathy among all people, reject tyrannical authority (God's authority), advocate practical common sense and justice, and be directed by the human conscience to undertake noble pursuits guided by the individual will."

If the Satanic Temple, which claims to be a religious order that seeks to encourage goodwill and empathy within the human race, then we must explore the basics of their beliefs and explore their doctrines in order to understand what motivates them. Listed below are seven fundamental tenets of the Satanic Temple:

1. One should strive to act with compassion and empathy towards all creatures in accordance with reason.

- Response: If humanity were driven by reason, then all of humanity would have understood by now the uselessness of tyranny, unfairness, murder, deception of all kinds and greed. Therefore, an appeal to reason is not sufficient enough to resolve humanity's innate problems. Paul said, "For I know that in me (that is, in my flesh,) dwelleth no good thing: for to will is present with me; but *how* to perform that which is good I find not" Rom. 7:18 (see also Matt. 15:19; Mar. 7:21-23).

2. The struggle for justice is an ongoing and necessary pursuit that should prevail over laws and institutions.

- Response: Who or what defines the justice that is to supersede the laws and institutions? Paul said, "What shall we say then? *Is* the law sin? God forbid. Nay, I had not known sin, but by the law: for I had not known lust, except the law had said, Thou shalt not covet" Rom. 7:7. Justice must never remain relegated to subjectivity.

3. One's body is inviolable, subject to one's own will alone.

- Response: This statement is a direct reflection of Aleister Crowley's statement, "Do what thou wilt," also known as the law of Thelema, which is from a book written by Crowley. Such a statement simply promote liberalism and lawlessness. Within this frame of thought, the totality of an individual is solely subject to their determinations alone and no other. This doctrine violates principles like Gal. 6:1, which requires us to be accountable to our fellowman.

4. The freedoms of others should be respected, including the freedom to offend. To willfully and unjustly encroach upon the freedoms of another is to forgo your own.

- Response: Paul goes as far as to say, "If eating certain things offends my fellowman, then I won't eat that thing" (1 Cor. 8:13). This is the heart of genuine respect, when people willingly sacrifice their pleasures in order to not offend or be a stumbling block for another (Rom. 14:21). Also, such a tenet violates the principle of love outline in 1 Cor. 13:4-5, when Paul said that love does not boast of oneself or selfishly put their desires above another.

5. Beliefs should conform to our best scientific understanding of the world. We should take care never to distort scientific facts to fit our beliefs.

- Response: This tenet appears to be self-contradicting because they profess to conform to "their" understanding of science. Science by definition is the intellectual and practical activity encompassing the systematic study of the structure and behavior of the physical and natural world through observation and experiment, and yet, they worship and promote an intangible supernatural being. When did the existence of Satan become a scientific fact?

6. People are fallible. If we make a mistake, we should do our best to rectify it and resolve any harm that may have been caused.

- Response: This statement serves as an admission that humans are imperfect, do possess imperfect reasoning, and therefore require a moral law such as found in the Bible (Rom. 1).

7. Every tenet is a guiding principle designed to inspire nobility in action and thought. The spirit of compassion, wisdom, and justice should always prevail over the written or spoken word.

- Response: What is the moral code that helps one determine nobility, compassion or justice? Without a moral code, like the Bible, will guiding principles remain discretionary or subject to the will as outlined in the mission? What if the will of one person fundamentally violates the will of another? If the human consciousness of someone's noble pursuits violate the individual will of another, do both still remain as noble pursuits?

Conclusion

Groups like the Satanic Temple profess themselves as being an atheistic-religious organization, rendering their fundamental beliefs self-contradictory. Elements of Luciferianism are also found in Masonic teachings, Wicca, and New Age philosophy. Because there is no agreed-upon code of beliefs, Luciferian beliefs are extremely varied.

Despite all of Satan's deceptions, Isaiah said this of his outcome, "Yet you will be brought down to hell, to the sides of the pit. [16.] Those that see you will narrowly look upon you, *and* in considering you will say, *Is* this the man that made the earth tremble and caused kingdoms to shake. [17.] Who made the world as a wilderness, and destroyed the cities thereof; *that* did not open the house of his prisoners?" (Isaiah 14:15-17).

Notes

SCIENTOLOGY

"THE DOCTRINE OF L. RON HUBBARD"

Scientology is a religion that professes to offer a precise path leading to a complete and certain understanding of one's true spiritual nature. It also claims to provide information on one's relationship to self, other individuals, other life forms, the material and immaterial universe, and their theory of God.

HISTORICAL BACKGROUND

Scientology was founded in Tilden, Nebraska in 1955 by Lafayette Ron Hubbard (1911-1986). According to Scientology history, by the age of 19, Hubbard had travelled over a quarter of a million miles through Eastern countries like China and India.

In 1950, Hubbard published *Dianetics: The Modern Science of Mental Health*, which became a text for the religion of scientology. His religion combines the psychoanalysis of Freud, Eastern thought, and ideas from his science fiction writing. The doctrine of Scientology is that the mind is divided into analytical and reactive segments. Hubbard's writings and recorded spoken words on the subject of Scientology collectively constitute Scientology's scripture.

DOCTRINE

In Scientology, the concept of God is expressed as the Eighth Dynamic, a concept derived from L. Ron Hubbard's "Science of Survival" stating:

"No culture in the history of the world, save the thoroughly depraved and expiring ones, has failed to affirm the existence of a Supreme Being. It is an empirical observation that men without a strong and lasting faith in a Supreme Being are less capable, less ethical and less valuable to themselves and society....A man without an abiding faith is, by observation alone, more of a thing than a man."

Scientology does not ask its members to accept anything on faith; rather, as spiritual awareness increases through participation in auditing and other training methods, one can attain personal clarity of each dynamic. According to Scientology, only when members have reach the seventh dynamic, then they can fully understand the eighth dynamic and one's relationship to the Supreme Being.

Scientology identifies the person as a spirit (*Thetan*)—not the body or mind—and believes that each individual is far more than their physical anatomy. Principal creeds among Scientologist are:

1. *Man is an immortal spiritual being.*
2. *Humanity's experience extends beyond an individual lifetime.*
3. *Individual capabilities are limitless.*

Scientology also holds that one's salvation depends on self and the fulfillment of uniting with the universe. Scientology does not require the acceptance of anything on faith alone, but rather seeks freedom through spiritual enlightenment.

How does Scientology work?

The Scientology religion seeks to aid its adherents in reaching a state of enlightenment, called "clear," where harmful sub-conscientious thoughts can be wiped out. Scientologist conduct powerful motivational processes called Auditing, which are sessions using a technology that L. Ron Hubbard designed to help "free" the human spirit. Auditing is the process of asking specifically worded questions designed to help the individual find and handle areas of anguish. This process is done with an auditor. Auditor is defined as "one who listens," from the Latin word *audire* meaning "to hear or listen; a listener," similar to a Life Coach. Unlike a licensed professional counselor, Auditors don't offer solutions or advice, they merely aid the "Pre-clear" (a person not yet clear) in self-exploration. During these sessions, Auditors might use standard Scientology technology called a Hubbard Electro-Psychometer (E-meter), believed to detect stress or a fluctuation in mood.

Controversy in Scientology

During an NBC News interview that aired January 17, 2013 Paul Haggis said, "Scientology is a cult." Haggis is an academy award-winning director, who was also a scientologist for over 30 years. When asked why he left the church, Haggis said, "I was ashamed of my own stupidity of how I could have been so purposely blind for so many years." Haggis later said that anyone in a group such as that chooses to be blind. When asked if Scientology helped him any, he said yes, but correlated it to a good self-help book. He said, "It's like picking up any good self-help book. You're going to get something out of it."

When asked about Scientology's enticement of people, Haggis

said, "There are things that actually help you. They help you get along a little better with your [spouse]. They help you understand your boss a little better. If there was something that didn't help you in your life, then it wouldn't get a hold of you." In other words, Scientology has nothing to offer that is everlasting. Though it has component that may be helpful for the participant, it is only temporal. Jesus said, "For God so loved the world that he gave his only begotten Son, that whosoever believeth in him should not perish, but have everlasting life." (John 3:16, KJV). Scientology can offer no such thing.

During a controversy regarding Proposition 8. Haggis initiated his own investigation about the internal affairs of the organization and discovered allegations of physical abuse and involuntary confinement among the churches highest levels. Haggis resigned from the church in 2009. Haggis is now associated with Lawrence Wright's new book entitled, "Going Clear: Scientology, Hollywood, & the Prison of Belief," which is based on Wright's investigation of the church, including interviews of over 200 people. Mostly of whom have professed to be former Scientology members.

Lawrence Wright was also interviewed by NBC. When he was asked about the church's controversial history, he said, "It has a history of being very vindictive and litigious. It has a history of infiltrating the government. Spying on people. So, it has created an atmosphere of fear that surrounds it." In the 1970's, the church launched a massive domestic espionage effort, called "Operation Snow White," because the church believed that the government was collecting information that could be damaging to the church. Following an FBI raid, eleven Scientologist were arrested including Hubbard's wife. They were convicted of infiltrating numerous government agencies and stealing documents.

"VERY EARLY ONE MORNING in July 1977, the FBI, having been tipped off about Operation Snow White, carried out raids on Scientology offices in Los Angeles and Washington, DC, carting off nearly fifty thousand documents. One of the files was titled "Operation Freakout." It concerned the treatment of Paulette Cooper, the journalist who had published an exposé of Scientology, The Scandal of Scientology, six years earlier. After having been indicted for perjury and making bomb threats against Scientology, Cooper had gone into a deep depression. She stopped eating. At one point, she weighed just eighty-three pounds. She considered suicide. Finally, she persuaded a doctor to give her sodium pentothal, or "truth serum," and question her under the anesthesia. The government was sufficiently impressed that the prosecutor dropped the case against her, but her reputation was ruined, she was broke, and her health was uncertain. The day after the FBI raid on the Scientology headquarters, Cooper was flying back from Africa, on assignment for a travel magazine, when she read a story in the International Herald Tribune about the raid. One of the files the federal agents discovered was titled "Operation Freakout." The goal of the operation was to get Cooper "incarcerated in a mental institution or jail."[75]

During our own observations of this organization, we have examined how the organization treats those who apostatize from Scientology. Anytime someone has disclosed internal affairs and personal experiences they had while affiliated with the organization, Scientology releases very distasteful reactions in an attempt to discredit the informer.

Conclusion

Scientology is riddled with secrecy and deception. It combines a mixture of pseudoscience and falls within the realm of self-help theories. Scientologist deny the deity of Christ, and place all of their faith in the doctrine of L. Ron Hubbard.

Scientology

According to Scientology, Jesus is no more than an incarnation of a higher being, not a means of salvation. However, Christ' role as defined by Scripture is the supreme Ruler and Savior of humanity (John 3:16). The Scientologist believes Christ to be in high regard, but misunderstands or denies the full strength of His position and work. The Christian apologist should use this as a point of witnessing to the Scientologist. Again, under the aid of the Holy Spirit and thoroughly studying the relating scriptures is required to help elucidate the position and redemptive work of Jesus Christ.

"Who is the image of the invisible God, the firstborn of every creature: For by him were all things created, that are in heaven, and that are in earth, visible and invisible, whether they be thrones, or dominions, or principalities, or powers: all things were created by him, and for him: And he is before all things, and by him all things consist."

~ Colossians 1:15-17

SECTION II

"ADDRESSING ETHICAL ISSUES"

ABORTION

In 1973, the Supreme Court made a monumental decision about women's rights that even today echoes throughout modern history. Roe vs. Wade ruled that it was unconstitutional for states to ban abortions except to save the life of the mother. This decision affected abortions performed during the first trimester of a pregnancy. PBS's Highlights of Landmark Cases states that though this was not the most important of the Supreme Court's decisions, it is the "most recognized."[76]

Prior to Roe v. Wade, most states had very strict standards which restricted or banned abortions. These restrictions and bans were opposed by the challenges presented by the sexual revolution and the feminist movement of the 1960's.[77] Today, we are forty-two years past the landmark case. Our landscape in terms of abortion is heavily debated and often used as a means to discuss everything from a movement away from personal responsibility and the decline of family values. According to the Guttmacher Institute,[78] 21% (about one in every five) pregnancies end in abortion. In terms of demographics, Non-Hispanic white women account for 37% of all abortions, non-Hispanic black women for 36%, Hispanic women for 25% and the remainder, women of other races.[79] Of concern to those seeking to establish a Christian ethic for the issue of abortion is the fact that 37% of women obtaining abortions identify themselves as Protestants. [80]

What is Abortion?

So just what is abortion exactly? Abortion has a dictionary definition of deliberately terminating a pregnancy, usually before the embryo or fetus is capable of independent life.[81] When Roe v. Wade was passed in 1973, abortion did not extend past the first trimester. Today, we are seeing a move towards late-term abortions. Late term abortions are those cases where a pregnancy is terminated after the 20th week of development. The conversation about late term abortion brings to light the social viewpoint of life and when it begins. The perspective of the Scriptures will be disclosed later in this writing, but for sake of argument let us look at the statement made by Senator Barbara Boxer from California in 2010.

In a debate on the senate floor with Rick Santorum, Boxer states that life begins "when you bring the baby home."[82] This response was based upon the concept of choice. According to Boxer, the concept of choice should extend even outside of the womb and is only invalidated when the baby is taken from the hospital to its home. We should note here that Senator Boxer's sentiments are extreme, but reflect a growing ideology about the lives of the unborn. Boxer is not an unlearned individual. She represents her state as a senator elected by her constituency. In the name of pro-choice, she chooses to allow the life of a child to be terminated, not because of harm to the mother, but because of the choice the mother has made. This is the growing definition of abortion. A definition that is skewing the lines of what secular society has called abortion to something more identifiable with infanticide.

What is Human Life?

There is a stale worn-out debate among pro-abortion activist and supporter about the definition of human life and when it begins in the womb. Instead of seeking the bias of any person, we considered it most appropriate to consult the only manuscript from the creator of all that is living, the Bible. According to the Bible, any fetus that could potentially survive a female womb is regarded as living. When we consider the question, "Is an unborn person less important than a conceived person?" we must note that God even calls our children His own: "You took your sons and daughters whom you bore to Me and sacrificed them...You slaughtered My children" (Ezekiel 16:20-21). Lynn Copeland in her text, "What God's Word Says About Abortion," states, God speaks very clearly in the Bible on the value of unborn children. God's Word says that He personally made each one of us, and has a plan for each life. With this in view, let us see what the Scriptures have to say about life and the value of this life even while in the womb.

A Purview of Life and the Womb

"Before I formed you in the womb I knew you, before you were born I set you apart" (Jeremiah 1:5). When God speaks to the prophet Jeremiah, He speaks in terms concerning Jeremiah's status in the womb. Before the formation of this prophet in the womb of his mother, God states that He knew, or had intimate, specific knowledge of who Jeremiah is and what He would accomplish. From this fact we can assert that God cares and considers the child in the womb to be significant. For God, the child forming in the womb has purpose and is distinct from any other individual. Unlike the sentiment of pro-choice supporters that posit the forming fetus or embryo as an extension of the woman's body, God sees a life that has predisposed purpose to impact the world. "Even before I was born, God had chosen me to be His" (Galatians 1:15).

Paul in Galatians 1:5 continues the concept of God having purpose for the unborn prior to birth. A child is esteemed as chosen by God, according to Paul. It is not customary to choose something or someone that is not living or merely an insubstantial product of a sexual liaison. Gestation and the subsequent birth is to God an act of generating new life and such life is considered important and of worth to God. "For You created my inmost being; You knit me together in my mother's womb . . . Your eyes saw my unformed body. All the days ordained for me were written in Your book before one of them came to be" (Psalm 139:13, 16). "Your hands shaped me and made me...Did You not clothe me with skin and flesh and knit me together with bones and sinews? You gave me life" (Job 10:8–12).

These passages from the poetic books of Job and Psalms use strong language to disclose God's view of the unborn. Psalm 139:13, 16 uses such words as "knit" and "unformed" in its descriptions to discuss the significant creation of the unborn. This unborn child is also described as being "shaped", "clothed with skin", and "knit" with "bones and sinews" to show how God has made people based upon His handiwork. This phenomenon is defined by Job 10:12 as the giving of life. "This is what the Lord says—He who made you, who formed you in the womb" (Isaiah 44:2).

God forms a living entity in the womb. Because man is made in God's own image (Genesis 1:27), each life is of great value to God: "Children are a gift from God" (Psalm 127:3). The Bible says of our Creator, "In His hand is the life of every living thing and the breath of every human being" (Job 12:10). God, the giver of life, commands us not to take the life of an innocent person: "Do not shed innocent blood" (Jeremiah 7:6); "Cursed is the man who accepts a bribe to kill an innocent person" (Deuteronomy 27:25). "You shall not murder" (Exodus 20:13). Taking the life of the unborn is clearly murder—"He didn't kill me in the womb, with my mother as my grave" (Jeremiah 20:17) — and God vowed to punish those who "ripped open the women with child" (Amos 1:13). "Did not He who made me in the womb make them? Did not the same One form us both within our mothers?" (Job 31:15).

The unborn child was granted equal protection in the law; if he lost his life, the one who caused his death must lose his own life: "If men who are fighting hit a pregnant woman and she gives birth prematurely but there is no serious injury, the offender must be fined . . .But if there is serious injury, you are to take life for life" (Exodus 21:22, 23). Life is a gift created by God, and is not to be taken away by abortion. God is "prochoice," but He tells us clearly the only acceptable choice to make: "I have set before you life and death, blessings and curses. Now choose life, so that you and your children may live" (Deuteronomy 30:19).

EUGENICS

The set of beliefs and practices that seeks to improve the quality of life in terms of human population and quality is called eugenics. Eugenics was a "science" made popular by Sir Francis Galton. The term "eugenics" was coined to describe the processes applied for improving the quality of human beings born into the world. Galton had read his half-cousin Charles Darwin's theory of evolution, which sought to explain the development of plant and animal species, and desired to apply it to humans. Galton believed that desirable traits were hereditary based on biographical studies.[83]

Eugenics as a practice has been in existence notably since the ancient Greek empire.[84] The practice has been found in modern times with programs in both the United States and Great Britain in the 20th century. The Nazi regime at the Nuremberg trials for war crimes cited the forced sterilization programs of the United States as similar to their efforts at genocide of the Jews during World War II. Yet, how is this significant to the discussion on abortion?

Eugenics is identified by Emeritus Professor of Psychology at the University of Ulster in Northern Ireland, Robert Lynn, as having two main categories, classical and new. Abortion actually falls under the classical category and is further identified as a negative form of eugenics to "[provide] information and services for the reduction of unplanned pregnancies and births."[85] A key figure in the provision of abortion services was Margaret Sanger. Sanger coined the term "birth control" and is well-known for her work in developing the American Birth Control League in 1921, a precursor to today's Planned Parenthood Federation of America.[86] She is noted for her active work in the women's reproductive rights movement. Sanger's grandson, Alexander Sanger, chair of the International Planned Parenthood Council, explained, "She believed that women wanted their children to be free of poverty and disease, that women were natural eugenicists, and that birth control, which could limit the number of children and improve their quality of life, was the panacea to accomplish this."[87]

If this concept of "women are natural eugenicists" holds true, then abortion statistics for our country alone are alarming, especially in light of Planned Parenthood's involvement with abortions in the U.S. Based upon a National Health Statistics Report done by the Centers for Disease Control, non-Hispanic Black women accounted for 36.2% of all abortions in the United States in 2011.[88] Non-Hispanic white women account for 37.2%, making non-Hispanic black and white women the two largest groups in the U.S. However, if we consider the fact that non-Hispanic blacks only account for 13% of the U.S. population, this is a substantial amount. Considering further that the largest provider of abortion in America are clinics with 93% of all abortions being performed there.[89] The largest operator of clinics for women's reproductive health issues in the U.S. is Planned Parenthood, making them the largest provider of abortion-related services with 15 to 37% of its funding going toward the approximately 330,000 abortions it performs each year.[90] With this information it is right to ask if some of the motivation for abortion is based upon thinning out undesirable components of the population, especially considering that God creates everyone in His image and likeness for a unique purpose. These are all considerations we must ponder when we view the world's interpretation of the abortion debate. For God, there is no debate, as the Scriptures clearly indicate that all life (defined as such at conception) is valuable.

Conclusion

The issue of abortion is more than about choices. It is an issue of defining the contents of the womb. The Bible declares that the contents of the womb are a life, while popular, secular opinion would have you believe that these contents are an extension of the woman's body and therefore subject to the desires of the individual. Doctors Tim McClinton and Roy Hawkins (2009) in their book, "Biblical Counseling," state that, "A [woman] with an unplanned pregnancy [need] to understand that the 'quick and easy' choice *is neither quick nor easy* but will carry repercussions for the rest of her life" (p. 13). McClinton and Hawkins go on to note that there are "side effects" from the trauma of an abortion such as depression and sleep disorders. Though this may not be the case for everyone, it does point to something that we seem to know without an ounce of Scripture or the viewpoint of a scientific study, there is something significant about what is produced in the womb.

As believers we must understand that those opinions and viewpoints contrary to the conviction provided by the Scriptures are no more than myths about what abortion is and the ultimate outcomes of having such a procedure. Secular society will tell the woman a thing like abortion is "a simple procedure" or that the fetus to be aborted is "not a baby". We have presented some information here that shows otherwise. Apart from the Scriptures, research is finding the Biblical record to be true. We are to understand that upon conception there is a life in the womb, that life has purpose, and God orchestrates the life that is created. It is God's standard, not our opinion, that should dictate the purpose and extent of a life.

Notes

MARRIAGE

"Marriage is two imperfect people committing themselves to a perfect institution, by making perfect vows from imperfect lips before a perfect God."

~ Myles Munroe

In order to properly define anything, it is important to understand first who created the thing in question, its true purpose, and the function for which it is most effective. For this section, the marriage discussion will center upon its creation, purpose, and function, along with additional applications to relate the information.

- Marriage is an entity created by God (Genesis 2:18-24; Matthew 19:4-6; Mark 10:6-9)
- Marriage is a law with consequences (Romans 7:2)
- Marriage is an institution (Hebrews 13:4)
- Marriage is the disclosure of the mystery between Christ

and the church (Ephesians 5:31-32)

- Marriage is a covenant vow made between a man and a woman in the presence of God (Ecclesiastes 5:4-7)

The marriage covenant

Covenant is a mutual agreement or consent of two or more persons to forbear some type of act or thing. Its word origin denotes coming together and agreement of thinking or reasoning.

- A covenant is valid only at the death of the testator (Hebrews 9:16-20)
- The marriage covenant is grounded in consummation of the relationship (Deuteronomy 22:13-17)
- The marriage covenant is a cord of three strands God, man and woman (Ecclesiastes 4:9-12)
- Ultimately, covenant represents final, irrevocable commitment (see the life of Abraham)

Love

There are four main Greek definitions of love: Storge (affection), philia or philos (relational or familial), eros (physical or sexual), and agape (indescribable, self-sacrificial). Agape is the type of love one should strive for in the marriage relationship.

- Description of love and its attributes (I Corinthians 13)
- Agape is expressed to others (I John 4:7-8, 18-21)
- Agape is a fruit of the Spirit (Galatians 5:22-23)
- Agape is expressed by God (Romans 5:8)
- Husbands are commanded to love as Christ loved the church (Ephesians 5:25-28)

Submission and sacrifice

- All are called to submit (Eph. 5:21, I Peter 5:5; Heb. 13:17)

- Failure to submit is rebellion and invokes consequences (1 Sam. 15:23)
- Man failing to submit to God's ordinances relating to treatment of the wife (Psalm 66:18; Malachi 2:13-14; I Pet. 3:7)
- Jesus is our model for submission (I Cor. 11:3; Phil. 2:5-10)

Intimacy

- Intimacy between a husband and wife is outlined in the Bible as fulfilling four areas: Procreation, recreation, communication, and release. (Genesis 1:28; Deuteronomy 7:13-14; Psalm 127:3-5; Proverbs 5:18-19; Song of Solomon 4:10-12)

Communication

Principles for effective communication are work on listening, think before speaking, tell the truth, and avoid unconstructive criticizing (James 1:19; Proverbs 18:13; Proverbs 15:28; Eph. 4:15; Ps. 34:13)

MARRIAGE PRINCIPLES

God created marriage

There is often a misconception that God is averse to sex and its expression. This is contrary to the Biblical record as it is outlined from the beginning. In the creation of mankind, God's making or building of Adam's help meet clearly showed God as the author of marriage and also signified His purpose for marriage (Genesis 2:18-23).

God's original intent for marriage was between man and woman

The LORD God intended for marriage to be between one man and one woman for life. Modern configurations of marriage that are contrary to this arrangement are not only contra-biblical, but also harmful to family. God arranged for the man and woman to come together as evidenced from their ability to pro-create upon consummation of the relationship. The very design of the man is complementary to the woman and that of the woman to the man. As we violate this standard principle, we also go against what nature has intended through God's original design (Genesis 2:24).

God intended man and wife to function as one

Jesus Christ only explains one configuration for marriage. When approached by the religious leaders of His day a question about marriage goes back to the core of creation and the intention of God within His creation. He speaks that marriage is put together by God in a joining of one man and one woman and that this joining of two is for the purpose of being one. As you view the Scriptures, it is important to note that there is no alternative pairing mentioned by Christ or any of the writers in the Old or New Testament. It is clear by what the Scriptures say, as well as what they do not say, that the intention of God was for one man and one woman to function as one in marriage (Matthew 19:4-6).

God intended the joining of man and wife to be put "asunder"

"What therefore God hath joined together, let not man put asunder." The definition of asunder in Greek is the word *chorizo*. Chorizo means to separate, divide, or depart. It was not God's intention for man and wife to only be joined together temporarily. God intended for the strength of covenant to be exhibited in the relationship between man and wife. Prefacing the conception of marriage given by Christ was the fact that Moses allowed a bill of divorcement because of the hardness of people's hearts. Marriage is a recognition of God's joining together a man and woman in a covenant relationship similar to God's relationship with believers (Mark 10:6-9).

Marriage is an honorable institution

We previously mentioned the extent of sexual immorality in a previous chapter. The institution of marriage must be held as honorable by all people whether married or not. There are consequences for our dishonoring of the marriage bed and the privileges that should be exclusive to marriage such as sex. Breaking the covenant of the marriage bed opens sex to all that are bold enough to engage in it. As long as marriage is held as an honorable institution it is a model for the covenant that God intended to have and develop with His people (Hebrews 13:4).

Marriage is a disclosure of the mystery concerning Christ the Bridegroom and His bride the church

Mysteries are disclosed to the initiated. God allows a man and woman to understand the extent of His love and care for the world and more specifically those that believe in His Son, Jesus Christ. As we experience marriage, we are ushered into the understanding of Christ and His church (Ephesians 5:31-32).

Marriage is a vow made between two people in the presence of God (Holy Matrimony)

Covenant is defined as a mutual agreement or consent of two or more persons to forbear some type of act or thing. Its etymology (word origin) derives the meaning of coming together and agreement of thinking or reasoning. In terms of God and marriage, covenant solidifies the promises made by God to man and is the strength of the marriage relationship. Because of the strength of emphasis of covenant in relationships, God's plan of redemption, relationship, and commitment towards man are interwoven through His Word, giving mankind hope and direction within horizontal and vertical interactions (Ecclesiastes 5:4-7). The biblical definition of Covenant in Greek is diatheke, which means an arrangement, a disposition of ones earthly possessions, to take effect upon the death of the individual; a testament or will.

Marriage is a Covenant

Covenants are established by the shedding of blood. In the marriage relationship the shedding of blood is typified in the physical intimacy between man and wife. Scripture has two ways of denoting covenant relationship as opposed to relationships outside of an established relationship in terms of sexual intercourse. The bible uses "know" to denote a man and woman in covenant relationship. The term "lie" is used to refer to a man and woman not in covenant relationship *(Hebrews 9:16-20)*.

Consummation and the blood

In OT times, there was a component of business attached to the joining of a man to a woman. The woman's father had to agree to the terms of engagement, which often meant an exchange of resources between parties. There was generally a lengthy betrothal period prior to the wedding. Brides waited for their groom at this time, preparing and purifying themselves for their bridegroom (example Esther's preparation). During this time the bride had to keep herself pure from the pressures of premarital relations. Proof of her virginity on the wedding night was commensurate with the evidence of blood upon the sheet of the bed the bride and bridegroom consummated upon *(Deuteronomy 22:13-17)*.

God's purpose for sexual intercourse was a means to establish the covenant between man and woman. There are physical, emotional, and spiritual implications to having sex outside of the confines of marriage. God's definition of one flesh is seen clearly in the verses presented as solidified through the sexual act. It is therefore vital that this vehicle of physical intimacy be confined to the marriage relationship *(Genesis 3:16, 1 Corinthians 6:13-15)*.

A Cord of Three Strands

Ecclesiastes 4:9-12 gives us an allegorical interpretation of the marriage relationship. Every marriage is only as successful as it incorporates the principle found in the allegory of the threefold cord. The three strands discussed here are the man, woman, and God. The bond which intertwines these three is covenant. In rope making, the strongest rope is one made with three cords. This is due to the fact that this number is the largest in which all cords can touch one another and the smallest for which the pressure, tension, and additional changes can be endured for which the rope is designed. Marriages as God intended have a relief system for the pressures, trials, hardships, and disputes that occur within such a relationship. However, it is within the confines of the marriage covenant that this relief is experienced.

THE NATURE OF COVENANT

Covenant is the basis of relationship

One of the definitions of covenant from the terms discussed earlier was a word called agreement. Agreement can be defined as harmony between parties or a union of minds upon a common goal or direction. The prophet Amos posed a question about agreement in his writing.

Marriage

Agreement is vital to establishing the stipulations of the covenant relationship both before and during the relationship. This establishes the standards by which financial decisions are made, what is considered hurtful, or if there are any lofty expectations a marriage partner or potential marriage partner is seeking from the relationship (*Amos 3:3*). Marriage is an institution established by God Himself (Gen. 2:18, *Mark 10:6-9*). It is vital that covenant partners remember that God created marriage to exhibit the mystery of Christ and His bride, the church (*Ephesians 5:31-32*).

Covenant is established by sacrifice

When God established His covenant with Abraham, He set a transcendent precedent for how a covenant is to operate. In Genesis 15, Abraham entered into a covenant with God through sacrificing a series of different types of animals symbolizing different components of the covenant established. In like fashion, the marriage covenant requires sacrifice from both parties. Recall that a true covenant is not enacted unless there is a death of the testator (Hebrews 9:16).

Represents final, irrevocable commitment

Due to the commitment Abraham made with God through covenant, he was willing to give up his most prized possession to keep the terms of his agreement. This gives us the extent to which we keep the covenant relationship intact. This type of resolve is what must be considered prior to committing one's life to an individual "til death do us part." If already in a relationship, we must do as Abraham did in Genesis 15 and drive the hindering forces and spirits away from our relationship and make it work. Note in Genesis 15 that God made Abraham responsible for driving the birds away, meaning God had already provided everything Abraham needed to do such a task.

'What is love?' is a deep philosophical question that has

plagued the most brilliant of minds throughout the ages. Amidst the confusion of a clear definition of love, many individuals have entered into a relationship on the premise of love only to find it to be like the wind, felt but, ultimately, intangible. Two individuals in a relationship can both say I love you, yet mean completely different things. Case in point, contingent on the type of love being expressed, love can mean friendship, or a love one has for a child as a mother, or the love two individuals physically attracted to one another may feel. Thus it is of vital importance that love be defined in all its dimensions and applied to the institution of marriage accordingly in the correct context.

LOVE

Love and its definition is always a topic of debate whether one is a scholar or individual discussing the complexity of it in conversation. Webster's 1828 Dictionary of the American Language defines the verb form of love as *to be pleased with; to regard with affection, on account of some qualities which excite pleasing sensations or desire of gratification.* This broad definition applies to the context of an individual stating that they 'love' someone's hairstyle or a type of food or a puppy or even another person.

As a noun, love is defined by Webster's 1828 Dictionary of the American Language as *an affection of the mind excited by beauty and worth of any kind, or by the qualities of an object which communicate pleasure, sensual or intellectual. It is opposed to hatred. Love between the sexes, is a compound affection, consisting of esteem, benevolence, and animal desire. Love is excited by pleasing qualities of any kind, as by kindness, benevolence, charity, and by the qualities which render social intercourse agreeable. In the latter case, love is ardent friendship, or a strong attachment springing from good will and esteem, and the pleasure derived from the company, civilities and kindness of others.*

Between certain natural relatives, love seems to be in some cases instinctive. Such is the love of a mother for her child, which manifests itself toward an infant, before any particular qualities in the child are unfolded. This affection is apparently as strong in irrational animals as in human beings.

However, definitions such as these give an underlying meaning that love is purely emotional in nature and therefore often outside of our will and control. Affection as we will see later is emotional in origin and often as flippant as the feeling such emotion can invoke. The love in the marriage institution is indeed defined at times by affection, but the strength of such love isn't reliant on affection alone, but the full scope of the definition of love which is affection, friendship, physical/emotional, and self-sacrificing.

Love as affection

Storge is the Greek term for affection. Affection is closely related to what we know as agape, but falls short due to the lack of self-sacrifice often found in storge. Affection generally doesn't have a choice in who it is directed towards since it is due to relation. For instance, mankind sees it as natural for an individual to have affection towards their own child. The natural relation between parent and child is common even amongst most animals. Friendships have their own level of affection, but again due to relation. It is only natural that a true friend would exhibit some type of affective response toward a friend. Though it is an affection based on relation, it is most often used as a descriptor for love between a parent and child. It falls short of the highest form of love since it gives 'love' and does not consider if it is truly meeting the needs of those this type of love is directed towards. Storge is a medium for the other loves to be described in this lesson.

Love as friendship

Philia is a love best described as friendship. In John 21 the extent of this type of love is exemplified in the conversation between

Jesus and Simon Peter. Jesus asks Peter, "Do you love me (with a self-sacrificing love)." Peter's reply three times is, "Yes Lord, I love you (I have an affection for, a relationship as a friend with you)."

Love as sexual

Eros is the Greek name of the popular Valentine's Day icon Cupid. As the son of Aphrodite, the goddess of love, Eros would cause individuals to become physically attracted to one another. All myths aside, eros is the general term often used by Greek authors such as Homer to describe love between a man and woman. This being the highest form of love understood by the Greek scholars, it was often portrayed in Greek society in the art of the day and the commonplace practice of pederasty amongst tutors and their protégés. Ancient Greece is known for their pervasive loose morality attributed directly to this understanding of love as eros. Even in modern Western culture, eros is often the epitome of love, to the detriment of what can truly be defined as pure, true love.

Love as selfless or self-sacrificing

Agape is the selfless, self-sacrificing love described in the Bible as the type of love God extends to mankind. The depth of this definition is so intriguing that Greek authors did not use it when trying to describe love. The use of agape is exclusive to the New Testament.

SUBMISSION

Submission in marriage seems to always be a topic of disdain for women and cause for joy amongst men. Though discussed in the Bible in reference to the marriage relationship, submission is still understood for those that have been married for months, years, and even decades. The purpose of today's session is to provide clarity as to the definitions, scriptural references, and application of this entity called submission.

Submission is often thought to be negative and synonymous with treatment similar to a doormat. However, any individual in the Bible that had power with God to manipulate the Earth realm was submissive. The definition of submission is to yield to people, principles, and precepts placed in our lives as authorities. Failure to submit invokes the consequences of no longer having the umbrella of protection of authority. One author used this illustration to explain submission: "A compact car and a semitrailer truck are traveling on the same stretch of highway. If both vehicles come upon a sign that says *right lane ends 500 feet merge left* and the truck is in a position in which it must merge, it must submit to the compact car or risk a collision. The truck is bigger, more powerful, and probably has some kind of important destination, but because of a set position, must abide by the laws of traffic and submission (yielding)" taken from *Liberated through submission* by P.B. Wilson.

All are called to submit. Married, unmarried, man, woman, boy, or girl everyone has to submit to someone (Eph. 5:21, I Peter 5:5; Heb. 13:17). Failure to submit is rebellion and invokes consequences (1 Sam. 15:23). Satan wanted to make himself like God *(Isaiah 14:12-15)*. In so doing, he neglected his position to go after a position he was never purposed or designed to fill. The true authority of any individual comes from their submission to the order established by God. Even the president must submit to the laws of the land and the rules he establishes while in office. If he rebels against set rules of engagement, conduct, and interaction he is rendered ineffective in his position. Someone better can take his position from him or he could go to prison. Likewise, a husband, though the head of the wife must abide by the principles established by the Word or face the consequences. God has established that a man that does not treat his wife appropriately will have his prayers hindered (Ps. 66:18; Malachi 2:13-14; I Peter 3:7).

Jesus is our model for submission

If Christ had not submitted, we would still be under the OT system of sacrifice for sin. Our submission to the authority in place is bigger than two individuals in a marriage. Recall, from earlier in the course that marriage between two people discloses the revelation of the mystery of Christ and His bride, the church (Psalms 66:18, Malachi 2:13-14, 1 Peter 3:7, (1 Corinthians 11:3, 1 Corinthians 11:3, Philippians 2:5-10).

The man's role in submission

A husband is to:

- Be the head (final decision maker) of the wife (Eph. 5:22-24).
- Love his wife (Eph. 5:25)
- Be the spiritual leader of the home
- Live with his wife according to understanding how and why God made her.
- Guide and direct the wife regardless of defiance, stubbornness, and rebellion.
- Take responsibility for her spiritual condition (1 Peter 3:7).

The wife's role in submission

Wives are to submit to their own husbands as unto the Lord. The submissive married woman is a woman of faith, strength, and power. The submissive wife has a positive viewpoint of herself, not as the inferior, subservient being often depicted when speaking of submission. Because of her willingness to follow the leadership of her husband, a husband in his true role will seek the wise counsel and more fine-tuned intuitive skills of the wife in decision making and creation of a God inspired vision for the family (Ephesians 5:22-24, 1 Peter 3:1-6).

Problems in submission

- Husband refusing to accept the responsibility of being the head or of submitting to God.
- Wife refusing to submit to the husband.
- In-laws or others outside the immediate family unit are allowed to influence the decisions of the family.
- The flesh – not the spirit – is dominant in the marriage relationship.
- John Maxwell says that one of the key indicators of leadership is that you have someone following you. As the head the husband will have to give an account of how he led his family (Hebrews 13:17). A man's leadership of his family and his wife, a wife's submission to her husband, cleaving to your mate, and walking in the Spirit are commandments for believers (I Cor. 11:3; Eph. 5:23; Eph. 5:22; Matt. 19:2-3; Gal. 5:16).

INTIMACY

Intimacy is often flippantly referred to as sex. As sex is indeed the act that is associated with the consummation of a marriage, is necessary for the reproduction of the species, and is referred to in scripture as a man "knowing" a woman, the true state of intimacy is deeper in scope and application. Anyone can have sex both inside of and outside of the marriage covenant. Crossing the line from a physical act to an intimate interchange requires the concept of becoming one flesh.

Webster's 1828 Dictionary of American English defines intimacy as *close familiarity or fellowship; nearness in friendship. Interacting with someone to whom the thoughts are entrusted without reserve or restraint.* In comparison, sexual intercourse is simply *a running or passing between sexes (more appropriately the male and/or female parts).* In the Bible there are two ways to describe when a man and woman are involved physically with one another. For acts of adultery, fornication, homosexuality, lesbianism, or any other sex act outside of marriage, sex is defined as lying with another individual (Genesis 19:32, Genesis 39:7, Exodus 22:16, Leviticus 18:20, 22-23, Leviticus 20:13).

The OT word for lie is *shakab* and in its simplest definition denotes no more than an occupation of the same space at the same time with no type of connection. When a man and woman are in a covenant relationship, the word used is "know." Knowing an individual invokes understanding, communication, and a relation and experience of the individual known. This word know in the original language is *yada*. Yada is used not only of relational and experiential intimacy in terms of man and woman, but also of God and man (Genesis 4:1, 17, 25).

Male viewpoint of intimacy

In expressing intimacy, men and women are wired differently. Men spell intimacy S-E-X. God created males with a strong drive. This drive is generated in the hypothalamus of the brain. Men can compartmentalize their lives and can therefore open a box and forget about other things going on in our lives. This is not the case with women. If one "box" is open, all boxes are open. Men find their masculinity in sexuality. Up to 90% of a man's feeling like a man feeling like a man is centered on sex. If a man experiences rejection from his wife sexually for any reason, understandable or not, he may shut down, pull away, or do something morally stupid. Too much rejection can cause a man to shut down emotionally and therefore stop meeting a vital need for his wife.

Female viewpoint of intimacy

Women spell intimacy T-A-L-K. Again, men and women are wired differently. While intimacy for men is physical, for women it is an emotional connection. Women require emotional closeness before anything can occur. Men can be visually aroused, but women need to be romanced and emotionally stimulated. For women to simply give in to a man's need for physical consummation without emotional connection makes her feel like a machine. The best analogy for these differences is to think of men as a stovetop and women as an oven. Men need little to no time to get aroused while women need time to warm up. Also, women do not compartmentalize aspects of their lives. If something is going on with the kids, if the house is a mess, if work/school has them stressed over a problem it will carry over into the bedroom if not addressed. Men must understand this difference since it is scriptural that we strive for understanding in this area (1 Peter 3:7).

Purpose of intimacy

Intimacy between a husband and wife is outlined in the Bible as fulfilling four areas: Procreation, recreation, communication, and release.

- Procreation is generating having children. In Genesis 1:28 and Deuteronomy 7:13-14, scripture lets us know that sexual reproduction is part of God's design (Genesis 1:28, Deuteronomy 7:13-14, Psalms 127:3-5).
- Recreation and release simply means that sex can be used as a means to relieve stress and pressure. Men often are more apt to use this means of relieving stress due to the

physical nature of sex and the release of endorphins causing a euphoric feeling. The Bible says that we should enjoy intimacy in the marriage relationship (Proverbs 5:18-19, Song of Solomon 4:10-12).

- Communication is an essential part to intimacy. In order to compensate for the deep differences between man and woman communication is required. Sex is no substitute for open and honest conversation. Where communication is encouraged and generated within a loving in environment, sex gives the level of intimacy and relationship that expresses what words cannot say. Scripture uses the concept of one flesh to allude to the communication component often missing in intimacy (Genesis 2:24).

What the bible says about intimacy

"Now concerning the things whereof ye wrote unto me: It is good for a man not to touch a woman. Nevertheless, to avoid fornication, let every man have his own wife, and let every woman have her own husband. Let the husband render unto the wife due benevolence: and likewise also the wife unto the husband. The wife hath not power of her own body, but the husband: and likewise also the husband hath not power of his own body, but the wife. Defraud ye not one the other, except it be with consent for a time, that ye may give yourselves to fasting and prayer; and come together again, that Satan tempt you not for your incontinency. But I speak this by permission, and not of commandment. For I would that all men were even as I myself. But every man hath his proper gift of God, one after this manner, and another after that. I say therefore to the unmarried and widows, It is good for them if they abide even as I. But if they cannot contain, let them marry: for it is better to marry than to burn" (1 Corinthians 7:1-9).

Communication

Amos 3:3 states, "Can two walk together, except they be agreed?" yet how does agreement occur? In order for two individuals to come to an agreement about something they must discuss how they will walk together, where they plan on going, and any other details that will make their trek successful. Beyond every other component discussed in the chapter so far, communication is probably the most important. Here, we will discuss the definition of communication, the difference between how men and women communicate, and last, the principles scripture gives us about communication.

Communication is the link that creates a relationship between people. It helps us to become who and what we are and also what we know. Communicating is either clear producing understanding or unclear producing confusion. When you communicate there are about six messages:

1. What you are trying to say
2. What you actually say
3. What someone hears
4. What someone thinks they hear
5. What someone says about what you said
6. What you think someone said about what you said

Therefore, based on this aspect alone, it is safe to conclude that communication is indeed hard work. Complicating this process further is that you communicate not just verbally, but with the tone of your voice and non-verbally as well. These three components must complement one another in order for a simple message to be delivered, and more importantly, received. Effective communication with all of these variables lies in the hearing of the listener. If they didn't get it the way you meant it, you have not communicated effectively.

The Male Communicator vs The Female Communicator

In the brain there is a bundle of nerves called the corpus callosum. The corpus callosum connects the right and left sides of the brain. In females, there are 40 percent more of these bundles and is responsible for quicker language development and reading skills. This connection also allows for an easier time "reading" someone's emotions, expressing feeling, and overall verbalizing. For males this difference makes for a need to develop spatial skills or action upon the thing thought as opposed to simple expression of feeling about it.

Tests at the University of Pennsylvania consisting of a series of brain scans between males and females found that females had more parts of their brain stimulated during communication. The conclusion of the study was that multiple sections of the female brain were on "call" at a particular time, while a male's brain was stimulated in only one section. This also explains the ability to "juggle" multiple task that the female possesses, while the male can read a magazine or watch a game on TV and be oblivious to the children, messy house, problems at work, or his wife's glaring stare of disapproval.

In communicating, this difference makes women more perceptive or intuitive, while men desire facts that they can process and understand. To frustrate the male further is the fact that females often have better sight, smell, hearing, and taste than males do. Boys, at early ages, ignore voices of parents and peers more often than girls due to an inability to drown out background noises and hear voices speaking to them effectively.

So, when do these differences collide? Because of how the female brain works if a problem arises she does not need to go through a sequence or linear model to solve the problem, while a man does. Males need order and structure and often will not accept a female's solution due to not completing the steps he deems necessary to solve the problem. Both parties must recognize this difference.

Another difference is the modes the male and female brains operate in. As discussed earlier men compartmentalize what goes on in their lives. Therefore, they operate in exclusive mode meaning they can exclude things at any time they deem unimportant to what they are focusing on, while women operate in a manner in which every aspect of their life is included or inclusive mode. Understanding this along with other differences that arise is a key in how we address our communication in the marriage relationship.

Communication in Scripture

The Bible is full of references as to how we should communicate. It also gives us instruction on the tongue and the mouth in terms of its operation so that we can speak correctly to everyone. The following is a group of references from scripture that give us vital principles in communicating effectively and responsibly.

- **Principle 1**: Work to be a good listener (James 1:19; Proverbs 18:13).
- **Principle 2**: Take your time to think responses through (Proverbs 15:28; 25:11; 29:20).
- **Principle 3**: Speak the truth in love (Ephesians 4:15, 25; 1 Peter 3:10).
- **Principle 4**: Build up your spirit man (heart) and work to protect and guard what is put in it (Matthew 12:34-35; Proverbs 4:23).
- **Principle 5**: Don't criticize (Psalms 34:13; Proverbs 12:18; 21:23; 29:20; James 3:5-10).
- **Principle 6**: Understand the differences between the male and female mind (1 Peter 3:7; Hebrews 12:14; Psalms 133:1).

Conclusion

Marriage is a gem. A diamond is not valuable because it is found in abundance and easily cultivated in a short period of time. The element that gives a diamond or any precious gemstone value is the time, pressure, heat, and the determination of the individual mining to search for the riches he knows exists within the rocks.

In like fashion, the individual seeking a marriage that will endure the test of time, pressure, fiery trial, temptation, mood swings, illness, hurt, and past pain can only accomplish such a task by searching within the ROCK. Knowing that a three-fold cord is not easily broken (Ecclesiastes 4:12), marriage must be solidified through the omnipotent power of Jesus Christ.

God intends for marriage to walk in the strength of the covenant it was meant to be. Marriage is not a contractual agreement, where two parties distrust one another and therefore establish rules of engagement in order to approach one another. But, rather it is an agreement established on trust, agreement, and death to one's personal intentions and aspirations to change the husband or wife. Understanding covenant as God intended helps us to walk in the fullness of the marriage relationship and then focus on our topic for next week, love.

As you begin to mature in your relationship with God and with your spouse you have a storge type love, an affection to the object of your love. Storge often says I love through obligation, often unknowingly, but with the ulterior, yet sincerely pure unction to find pleasure in supplying a need of yours. At times you may have a phileo type love, which says yes we have the most intimate form of relationship two people can have, yet you are my friend. On the physical level, eros is present, which says I have a physical attraction for you that causes my storge type love to express itself in a different way. Yet, in the midst of the other types of love, agape is a love that says I love you regardless of what you do, regardless of if it will kill or hurt me to do so, just because you need love the way you do. When all other types of love seem to be lost, it is agape that stands the test of time and pressure (I Corinthians 13:13). Therefore, it is agape that one should strive for in the marriage relationship. However, to truly love someone with agape, you must know the originator of such a love—God Himself.

Submission is a position of power since it subjects itself to the power found in God's provision. All are required to submit. Rebellion in submitting to established powers opens individuals to the harsh consequences of what such impunities entail. For a successful marriage, relationship with God, and empowered walk with God, submission is key.

Intimacy must be understood in terms of the differences God made between man and woman and the guidelines pointed out in the Word. Procreation, recreation, communication, and release are the essential components of intimacy and should not be neglected within a committed marriage relationship. We are admonished to keep sex in the confines of marriages since there are penalties for lack of restraint in the area of sex. Keeping in mind the scripture, purpose, and principles concerning intimacy are essential in making the marriage relationship flourish and grow through the many tests and trials such a relationship must undergo.

Men and women are different. We look, act, react, and communicate in different ways. However, it is possible for a man and woman in the marriage covenant to work on one accord. Communication is not just what you say, it is what the other person has heard. If we take the knowledge of the natural differences God has made man and woman to have in reference to each other and work towards being understood, we are well on our way to effective communication and a successful marriage that works as a functional apologetic to God's way to approach matrimony.

Overview of Marriage Scriptures

The following is an overview of basic scriptures concerning marriages. Marriage as a topic can be studied either as superficially or in-depth as an individual likes. This study will concisely exegete the following scriptures to provide clarity and understanding of marriage as it is disclosed in scripture:

Genesis 2:18-25

"And the LORD God said, It is not good that the man should be alone; I will make him a help meet for him." Help-meet is the Hebrew ay-zer neged meaning an *aid in purpose*. God made the woman an aid in the purpose of the mission given to man. This becomes important when scriptures discuss submission. Man must submit to God's intent for his life and the woman must then submit to the vision and purpose God has given the man (Genesis 2:18-25).

Proverbs 5:15-19

Solomon in this passage is dispersing wisdom concerning the marriage relationship. The verse listed entails fidelity in the sexual aspect of the relationship. Other scriptures lay the foundation for the covenant of marriage on the grounds of consummation. If one "lays" with someone outside of marriage it is sin and has consequences (as all sin does).

Matthew 19:4-6; Mark 10:5-9

Both passages from Matthew and Mark detail Christ speaking to the Pharisees and scribes concerning the topic of divorce. Before Christ goes into any discussion of what the law permits concerning divorce, he focuses on the original intent of God in the marriage covenant. His thoughts and discourse read directly from Genesis chapter 2 verse 24.

Ephesians 5:21-33

Submission and sacrifice are the focus of this passage. All are called to submit. Wives are commanded to submit to their own husbands and then given a description of the hierarchy in relationships. In addition, husbands are commanded to love their wives as Christ loved the church. The elements listed are needed in order to disclose the mystery of the relationship between Christ and the church.

Notes

SEXUAL IMMORALITY

The 1960's brought about a definitive time-period where a phenomenon known as the sexual revolution emerged. It was not that behaviors revealed to the general public were not practiced prior to the sexual revolution, but that they were more clandestine and hidden from general view. It was during the time of sexual revolution and liberation that behaviors outside of the normative male-female, monogamous, marriage relationship seemed to be under exploration. Along with this phenomenon were advances in medical science such as the birth control pill and penicillin, which made the consequences of promiscuous sexual practices less daunting. Sexual exploration outside of the marriage bed is the calling card of this revolution and therefore acts as a starting point for this part of the ethics section.

Sexual immorality deals with those practices related to sexual intercourse that go against conventional personal standards of right and wrong, which often are either permitted or not covered by a formal code of law. We use the word "often" here as some of these immoral practices do currently have laws dictating their inappropriateness in engagement, yet the codification of a law against certain behaviors still does not deter the practice of sexually immoral acts. Regardless of the expediency of a law or not, we will once again define some of the sexually immoral practices in light of the Scriptures. Our inquiry into sexual immorality will focus mainly on Leviticus 18 and 20, as well as Romans 1, but will begin with the first prohibition found in the Ten Commandments in Exodus 20. It is our prayer that this section will provide the reader with a Scriptural basis for right and wrong as it relates to this issue.

OVERVIEW

"After the doings of the land of Egypt, wherein ye dwelt, shall ye not do: and after the doings of the land of Canaan, whither I bring you, shall ye not do: neither shall ye walk in their ordinances. ⁴ Ye shall do my judgments, and keep mine ordinances, to walk therein: I am the LORD your God. ⁵ Ye shall therefore keep my statutes, and my judgments: which if a man do, he shall live in them: I am the LORD."

~ Leviticus 18:3-5

It is important to note that Israel upon their exodus from Egypt had to contend for a new mind that God attempted to give them. This new mind was to be distinct from their past in Egypt and their future as conquerors of the land of Canaan. Israel had a difficult time separating from the practices of both Egypt and Canaan falling repeatedly into idolatry often because of sexual sin practiced by the groups around them. The folly of Israel echoes today as we see great men and women, often leaders and respected pillars of society falling into wide diversities of sexual sin and immorality. These diversities will be covered here in brief.

This section will cover some of the aberrations to God's order for sex and sexuality. Without opinion, this section will unapologetically note what the Scriptures say about a topic and give its understanding. A conclusion will pull all elements discussed together into a concise, succinct view of what a Christian worldview is in light of the Scriptures. The aim of this passage is to define the Scriptural position and give evidence for the believer and non-believer alike for God's true purpose for sex and what occurs when we leave the confines of His parameters.

ADULTERY

"Thou shalt not commit adultery."

~ Exodus 20:14

Ashley Madison is an online social media site with the tagline, "Life is short, have an affair." A firestorm occurred when a hacker released the names and email addresses of the purveyors of the site. The aftermath was one of distrust, suspicion, broken homes, and in more extreme circumstances, suicide. The Ashley Madison situation does bring to light some substantial questions about the nature of marriage relationships and people's desire to go outside of these relationships to fulfill sexual urges. As we view Scripture, we see that things are made quite clear about God's view of the act of adultery. Let us begin with the code given to Moses to present to the children of Israel, the Ten Commandments. More specifically, the seventh commandment, "Thou shalt not commit adultery."

Adultery is when a married person breaks the fidelity of the marriage vow by voluntarily engaging in sexual intercourse with someone other than their spouse. The act of adultery is more than just an activity within the scope of God's supreme law which must be prohibited, it is also dissolution of the security of the family structure as God intended. Within the prohibition against adultery we are reminded that God had deeper purpose for individuals in marriage than just personal pleasure and fulfillment of desire.

God is very explicit in His command to not commit adultery. It is also interesting to note that this command seems to be the only one that clearly defines some type of illicit sexual relation. God begins with purpose and vision concerning mankind. The purpose and vision God sets is the boundary for how we were intended to function. Therefore, we can determine that God's purpose was for a man and woman to commit to each other fully and exclusively in a bond of marriage. This is further reiterated by the definition of adultery in Hebrew, *na'aph*, as breaking the wedlock. Marriage is to lock in place the commitment between men and women. From this solitary commitment between a man and woman the sexual relationship is supposed to stay. Once we venture outside of marriage in the act of adultery, we begin to see the multitude of expressions of sexual immorality. This showcases the importance of marriage and commitment to that marriage in the sexual union and the consequences when someone ventures outside of what God has instituted.

FORNICATION

Fornication is very simply sexual relations between people not married to each other. In the Old Testament fornication is rendered by the Hebrew term *zanah*. Zanah means to commit the act of prostitution or promiscuous activity. This term is also associated and used metaphorically for Israel's penchant for idolatry. Using the term prostitution in the definition of fornication makes this term more impactful. Prostitution is defined as the act or occupation of engaging in sexual activity with someone for payment. It is putting a price upon your body and leasing the body out to someone that can pay the price. In relation to the body being offered, the Apostle Paul gives us the understanding that, "Flee fornication. Every sin that a man doeth is without the body; but he that committeth fornication sinneth against his own body. What? Know ye not that your body is the temple of the Holy Ghost which is in you, which ye have of God, and ye are not your own? For ye are bought with a price: therefore glorify God in your body, and in your spirit, which are God's" (1 Corinthians 6:18-20).

Here, the New Testament word for fornication, *porneia*, is introduced. Porneia is again characterized by illicit or forbidden (outside the marriage union) sexual intercourse, prostitution, and idolatry. If we are to submit our body to anyone, it should be based upon God's terms. It states in the 20th verse of 1 Corinthians 6, that we are bought with a price. This means we are redeemed with something of proper value or of substantial honor. Committing fornication is a dishonoring of the body that Christ died to save by demeaning its value into the lusts and desire of someone unworthy of the value your body, whether male or female, contains.

INCEST & PEDOPHILIA

None of you shall approach to any that is near of kin to him, to uncover *their* nakedness: I *am* the LORD. 7 The nakedness of thy father, or the nakedness of thy mother, shalt thou not uncover: she *is* thy mother; thou shalt not uncover her nakedness. 8 The nakedness of thy father's wife shalt thou not uncover: it *is* thy father's nakedness. 9 The nakedness of thy sister, the daughter of thy father, or daughter of thy mother, *whether she be* born at home, or born abroad, *even* their nakedness thou shalt not uncover. 10 The nakedness of thy son's daughter, or of thy daughter's daughter, *even* their nakedness thou shalt not uncover: for theirs *is* thine own nakedness. **11** The nakedness of thy father's wife's daughter, begotten of thy father, she *is* thy sister, thou shalt not uncover her nakedness. **12** Thou shalt not uncover the nakedness of thy father's sister: she *is* thy father's near kinswoman. **13** Thou shalt not uncover the nakedness of thy mother's sister: for she *is* thy mother's near kinswoman. **14** Thou shalt not uncover the nakedness of thy father's brother, thou shalt not approach to his wife: she *is* thine aunt. **15** Thou shalt not uncover the nakedness of thy daughter in law: she *is* thy son's wife; thou shalt not uncover her nakedness. **16** Thou shalt not uncover the nakedness of thy brother's wife: it *is* thy brother's nakedness. **17** Thou shalt not uncover the nakedness of a woman and her daughter, neither shalt thou take her son's daughter, or her daughter's daughter, to uncover her nakedness; *for* they *are* her near kinswomen: it *is* wickedness.

18 Neither shalt thou take a wife to her sister, to vex *her*, to uncover her nakedness, beside the other in her life *time*. **19** Also thou shalt not approach unto a woman to uncover her nakedness, as long as she is put apart for her uncleanness (Leviticus 18:6-18).

Sexual relations between relatives too closely related to be married to one another is identified as incest. In a January 24, 2013, article in *The Atlantic* entitled, "America has an Incest Problem," statistics reveal one in every three to four girls and one in every five to seven boys under the age of 18 are victims of sexual abuse with an overwhelming amount of perpetrators being family members.[91] Recall, many of the controversies of the Roman Catholic Church or the Penn State sexual abuse of young boys under Coach Jerry Sandusky are not the norm in relation to the pervasiveness in incest cases. Within the *Atlantic* article, Mia Fontaine writes, "Child sexual abuse impacts more Americans annually than cancer, AIDS, gun violence, LGBT inequality, and the mortgage crisis combined."

The problem is that institutional abuses often talk about types of abuse that occur by individuals unfamiliar to victims. However, incest involving minors most often occurs within the family and is the first form of institutional abuse. Incest is a "notoriously underreported crime."[91] Because of the familial nature of the crime, cases of incest are often dealt with internally by families. This means that law enforcement will not impose the full extent of law and molesters are free to victimize again. This revolving door of molestation often results in multi-generational abusers as well as being more likely than non-victims to engage in varying degrees of risky sexual behavior.[93]

Since we are discussing the issue of adults involved sexually with children, we must introduce the formal definition of pedophilia. Pedophilia is considered to be a "paraphilia", an abnormal, unnatural sexual attraction. This paraphilia is characterized by sexual attraction to children through fantasy or activity. In relation to this paraphilia, most are found to be men.[94] According to Psychology Today, an estimated 20% of American children have been molested making pedophilia the most common paraphilia.

It is important to note that a Biblical view of sex and sexuality depicts improper sex and its various aberrations from the definitive norm of marriage between a man and woman as a resulting factor of a depraved heart.[95] Romans 1:24 discusses how God gave individuals in their depravity up to *uncleanness, in the lust of their hearts, to dishonor their bodies among themselves.* As mentioned in the previous section on fornication, we are to understand that the body which God created is sacred and *bought with a price.* We dishonor this sacredness in our engagement with sexual sin of any kind and this is all the more evident when a child is violated because of the lusts of an adult. The tenor of this argument will be repeated throughout this chapter.

HOMOSEXUALITY

22 Thou shalt not lie with mankind, as with womankind: it *is*

abomination" (Leviticus 18:22).

[18] For the wrath of God is revealed from heaven against all ungodliness and unrighteousness of men, who hold the truth in unrighteousness; [19] because that which may be known of God is manifest in them; for God hath shewed *it* unto them. [20] For the invisible things of him from the creation of the world are clearly seen, being understood by the things that are made, *even* his eternal power and Godhead; so that they are without excuse: [21] because that, when they knew God, they glorified *him* not as God, neither were thankful; but became vain in their imaginations, and their foolish heart was darkened. [22] Professing themselves to be wise, they became fools, [23] and changed the glory of the uncorruptible God into an image made like to corruptible man, and to birds, and fourfooted beasts, and creeping things. [24] Wherefore God also gave them up to uncleanness through the lusts of their own hearts, to dishonour their own bodies between themselves: [25] who changed the truth of God into a lie, and worshipped and served the creature more than the Creator, who is blessed for ever. Amen. [26] For this cause God gave them up unto vile affections: for even their women did change the natural use into that which is against nature: [27] and likewise also the men, leaving the natural use of the woman, burned in their lust one toward another; men with men working that which is unseemly, and receiving in themselves that recompence of their error which was meet. [28] And even as they did not like to retain God in *their* knowledge, God gave them over to a reprobate mind, to do those things which are not convenient; [29] being filled with all unrighteousness, fornication, wickedness, covetousness, maliciousness; full of envy, murder, debate, deceit, malignity; whisperers, [30] backbiters, haters of God, despiteful, proud, boasters, inventors of evil things, disobedient to parents, [31] without understanding, covenant breakers, without natural affection,

implacable, unmerciful: [32] who knowing the judgment of God, that they which commit such things are worthy of death, not only do the same, but have pleasure in them that do them" (Romans 1:18-32).

If ever there were a hot-button issue for our time, homosexuality holds the attention of our nation and world as it garners for the time of media outlets and the minds of those it crosses. Homosexuality concerns sexual activity between people of the same sex. The Centers for Disease Control tallied statistics in 2013 for the Lesbian, Gay, Bisexual, and Transgender population in the United States notes that only 2% of the population is identified as men who have sex with men.[96] A National Health Statistics Report from the CDC from 2013 specifically detailing the LGBTQ community identifies 1.6% of the population identifying as gay or lesbian and 0.7% as bisexual.[97] Another 1.1% identified themselves as "other", did not understand the question, or declined to answer the query into their sexual orientation. [98]

This section could easily go into a line by line refutation against arguments made by advocates of homosexuality. However, since this is a text on apologetics, we will discuss what the Bible says about the topic to equip the reader. In order to meet this end, we will examine the configuration that God sanctions for sexual relationship and how God views configurations contrary to this arrangement.

Using gay marriage as a standard of acceptance of the practice of homosexuality, we see a very interesting trend in mainline Christian denominations. According to the Pew Research Council, five out of the ten mainline Christian denominations are accepting of gay marriage with some of the five even sanctioning the performance of commitment ceremonies between two people of the same sex that plan to marry.[99] From this information it is evident that a clear stance against homosexuality is not being taken that is defined by the Scriptures.

Many, when seeking to refute the claim of Christianity in reference to homosexuality, state that Jesus Christ never spoke against homosexuality. Based on the original configuration that the LORD God established, Jesus spoke. In such a case there is no reason to discuss what an individual should not be doing. In reference to a question concerning marriage and divorce Jesus states, "⁶ But from the beginning of the creation God made them male and female. ⁷ For this cause shall a man leave his father and mother, and cleave to his wife; ⁸ and they twain shall be one flesh: so then they are no more twain, but one flesh. ⁹ What therefore God hath joined together, let not man put asunder. ¹⁰ And in the house his disciples asked him again of the same *matter.* ¹¹ And he saith unto them, Whosoever shall put away his wife, and marry another, committeth adultery against her. ¹² And if a woman shall put away her husband, and be married to another, she committeth adultery" (Mark 10:6-12).

If there were any other configuration, wouldn't Jesus have mentioned it here when speaking of a natural order of things? In defense of this fact of the Biblical record, individuals in support of homosexuality point to nature, animals, and the concept of committed relationship in the modern derivatives of homosexual relationship. Speaking of nature, everyone should understand that we are born in sin and shapen in iniquity (Psalm 51:5), so being born in a state of proclivity to an activity is not license to engage in it. Referencing animals as a basis for engaging in sinful activity is invalid as animals also may eat their young. We see no benefit in doing likewise (hopefully) so we don't condone such activity as acceptable. There is a choice involved in who we love. Using the concept of subjugation in previous centuries and millennia of homosexual relationship as a validation of the current state of commitment and mutual consent as a standard for rightness and rectitude also does not constitute God's way.

The Biblical record is clear in defining the boundaries of sexual relationship. Homosexuality should not be taken as a solitary entity in terms of sex and sexuality. It is a form of fornication and a violation of God's moral code. Further, it is defined as an abomination, meaning it is damaging to the person and the image (God's image) that is placed upon the individual. In all occasions of sexual sin we must remember to glorify God in our body and in our spirit (1 Corinthians 6:20), as they belong to Him.

BESTIALITY

" 23 Neither shalt thou lie with any beast to defile thyself therewith: neither shall any woman stand before a beast to lie down thereto: it *is* confusion" (Leviticus 18:23).

Bestiality is also known as zoophilia. It is the love (in a sexual manner) of animals. The Biblical definition of this activity calls it confusion. Confusion here is the Hebrew term tebel meaning violation of nature or divine order. The concept here is one of perversion due to sexual sin. Contemporary statistics are few on this topic and often are no more than conjecture due to the embarrassing nature of the act. Scriptures are clear as to the morality of bestiality and its position as a violation of God's order for sexual relationship.

PORNOGRAPHY

24 Defile not ye yourselves in any of these things: for in all these the nations are defiled which I cast out before you: 25 and the land is defiled: therefore I do visit the iniquity thereof upon it, and the land itself vomiteth out her inhabitants. 26 Ye shall therefore keep my statutes and my judgments, and shall not commit *any* of these abominations; *neither* any of your own nation, nor any stranger that sojourneth among you: 27 (for all these abominations have the men of the land done, which *were* before you, and the land is defiled;) 28 that

the land spue not you out also, when ye defile it, as it spued out the nations that *were* before you. ²⁹ For whosoever shall commit any of these abominations, even the souls that commit *them* shall be cut off from among their people. ³⁰ Therefore shall ye keep mine ordinance, that *ye* commit not *any one* of these abominable customs, which were committed before you, and that ye defile not yourselves therein: I *am* the LORD your God" (Leviticus 18:24-30).

Leviticus 18 covers all of the sexual sin that Israel either engaged in or were privy to in Egypt (their land of bondage) and upon entrance into Canaan (their land of promise). God admonishes the Israelites to not engage in the acts of the Egyptians or the Canaanites who were idolaters. Evidence of idolatry was often the occasion of temple prostitution and harlotry so that "worshippers" could experience the presence of a deity. It is obviously wrong to engage in sexual relations outside of the marriage bed, but what if you are not the one engaging in the act itself? Here enters the occasion of pornography. "³² who knowing the judgment of God, that they which commit such things are worthy of death, not only do the same, but have pleasure in them that do them" (Romans 1:32).

A document published by an organization called Covenant Eyes, Inc. entitled *The Porn Circuit* discusses the physiological and neurological components of viewing pornography.[100] The findings echo the words of Job in Job 31:1, "I made a covenant with mine eyes; why then should I think upon a maid? (Job 31:1).

Romans 1:32 speaks of individuals that have pleasure in those that engage in violations of God's order are actually worthy of His wrath. We must always remember that sin runs deeper than just personal pleasure or vice. Pornography is an excellent example of this fact. A website called familysafemedia.com has several interesting statistics about pornography that are important and relevant to share concerning this section.[101] Every 39 minutes a new pornographic video is being created in the United States. The pornography industry is larger than the revenues for Microsoft, Google, Amazon, and Apple. There are over 420 million pornographic websites in existence; meaning about 1 in every 10 sites has a pornographic theme. Eleven years old is the average age of first internet pornography exposure. Almost half of all Christians polled confirmed pornography as being a major problem in the home. Of all internet pornography visitors, the breakdown is 72% male and 28% female.

More significant is the amount of exploitation, human trafficking, and general sexual abuse occurs under the guise of harmless entertainment. According to UNICEF, 1.2 million children are being trafficked every year; this is in addition to the millions already held captive by trafficking. UNICEF also notes that every 2 minutes a child is being prepared for sexual exploitation and approximately 30 million children have lost their childhood through sexual exploitation over the past 30 years. The total market value of illicit human trafficking is estimated to be in excess of $32 billion Sex trafficking is the fastest-growing business of organized crime and the third-largest criminal enterprise in the world.[102] The majority of victims are taken from such places as South and Southeast Asia, the former Soviet Union, Central and South America, and moved to more develop ones, including Asia, the Middle East, Western Europe, and North America.[103] An estimated 293,000 American youths currently are at risk of becoming victims of commercial sexual exploitation. The majority of these victims are runaway or thrown-away youths who live on the streets and become victims of prostitution.[104]

These statistics are important in light of pornography since the activity associated with pornography and its production fuels the needs of the sex trafficking trade. As Christians we must advocate for moral sexual purity for the benefit of our personal well-being, our children, and for the millions of men, women, and children being exploited worldwide.

Conclusion

This concise list of sexually immoral activity by no means covers the wide gamut of activities associated with such sins. Christians are not exempt from sexual temptation and must be mindful to walk in a Scriptural conviction toward sin in general. A pure apologetic does not look outside of the Word of God to find understanding. The times in which we live seek to establish that those that operate within a Scriptural worldview are on the wrong side of history. You will hear that a lack of compromise with the tenor of the age is bigotry, old-fashioned, or even un-Christian. God calls us to moral purity, and the moral purity is based upon God's Word. Recall, the following general principles in our interaction with addressing a Biblical understanding of sexual immorality (1 Corinthians 6:9-10, 13-20):

1. Jesus Christ operates and speaks within the Gospels concerning the original purpose of mankind. Sexually immoral elements are not included within this understanding of God's purpose.

2. We don't engage in or take pleasure (approve) of sexual immorality. This means we must be mindful of areas where we may be co-signing with the world's system of sexual relationships.

3. The scope of sexual immorality and sin emerges from a depraved heart and is larger in impact than just one person's vice and pleasure as evidenced by the activity surrounding pornography.

As you seek to defend the Gospel of Jesus Christ and answer every man according to the hope that lies within you (1 Peter 3:15), always use the Bible as your primary guide and reference.

Notes

BIBLIOGRAPHY

1. Burke, D. (2015, April 3). The fastest growing religion in the world is ... - CNN.com. Retrieved from http://www.cnn.com/2015/04/02/living/pew-study-religion/
2. Groothius, 2011, p. 122
3. What is Worldview? https://www.youtube.com/watch?v=Txez9sJUtaE
4. Diederik Aerts, Leo Apostel, Bart de Moor, Staf Hellemans, Edel Maex, Hubert van Belle & Jan van der Veken (1994). "World views. From Fragmentation to Integration". VUB Press. Translation of (Apostel and Van der Veken 1991) with some additions. – The basic book of World Views, from the Center Leo Apostel. Retrieved March 12, 2015, from http://www.vub.ac.be/CLEA/pub/books/worldviews.pdf
5. What is a worldview? Retrieved March 12, 2015, from http://cogprints.org/6094/2/Vidal_2008-what-is-a-worldview.pdf
6. Polhill, J. (1992), p319. *The New American Commentary: ACTS.* Nashville, TN: Broadman Press. Pg. 77
7. "The Christian Broadcasting Network." The Baptism in the Holy Spirit: Spiritual Life in God. 2015. Accessed October 16, 2015. http://www.cbn.com/spirituallife/cbnteachingsheets/gifts_of_the_spirit.aspx. Para. 4
8. Walvoord, John F. "The Person of the Holy Spirit Part 7 The Work of the Holy Spirit in Salvation." *Bibliotheca Sacra* 98, no. 392 (October 1941
9. Vine's Complete Expository Dictionary of Old and New Testament Words by W.E. Vine., pg. 576-577
10. New Testament words by William Barclay ppg 118-125

11. Ibid, pg. 206-209
12. Ibid, pg. 268
13. The Complete Word Study Dictionary by Spiros Zodhiates
14. Jason J. Barker, 2005; http://www.orthodoxyouth.org/romans/print/introexpulsionjews.htm
15. http://www.pewforum.org/2011/12/19/global-christianity-exec/
16. http://www.bbc.com/news/magazine-24864587
17. https://www.opendoorsusa.org/christian-persecution/world-watch-list/
18. http://www.foxnews.com/entertainment/2015/08/13/john-rhys-davies-have-lost-our-moral-compass-completely/
19. https://www.opendoorsusa.org/christian-persecution/world-watch-list/wwl-faq/
20. Edwin Yamauchi, quoted in Lee Strobel, *The Case for Christ* (Grand Rapids, Michigan: Zondervan Publishing House, 1998), 82.
21. Tacitus, Annals 15.44, cited in Strobel, *The Case for Christ*, 82.
22. Some information about the estimated distribution of Protestants among these subgroups is provided in the section on Christian Movements and Denominations.
23. "Independents," in Todd M. Johnson and Kenneth R. Ross, editors, *Atlas of Global Christianity*, Edinburgh University Press, 2009, pages 76-77.
24. Watchtower, Official Web Site of Jehovah's Witnesses, *http://www.watchtower.org/e/jt/article_03.htm* and *http://www.watchtower.org/e/dg/article_09.htm*.
25. Watchtower, Official Web Site of Jehovah's Witnesses.
26. ChristianScience.com, owned and operated by The First Church of Christ, Scientist, and its affiliate, The Christian Science Publishing Society.
27. Jeffers, H. (2005). *Freemasons: Inside the world's oldest secret society.*

New York: Citadel Press.

28. Ibid., p. 10

29. Ibid., p. 10

30. Ibid., p. 1

31. Ibid., p. 2

32. Ibid., p. 2

33. Ibid., p. 2

34. Tolson, J. (2005, September 5). Inside the masons. *US News.* Retrieved June 24, 2006, from http://www.usnews.com/usnews/culture/articles/050905/5masons.htm

35. New Advent Catholic Encyclopedia. (2003). *Masons (Freemasonry).* Retrieved June 24, 2006, from http://www.newadvent.org/cathen/09771a.htm

36. Jeffers, H. (2005). *Freemasons: Inside the world's oldest secret society.* New York: Citadel Press.

37. Ankerberg, J., &Weldon J. (1989). *The facts on the Masonic lodge.* Eugene, OR: Harvest House Publishers.

38. C. Eric Lincoln, The Black Muslim in America, 3d. ed. [Grand Rapids: Wm. B. Eerdmans Publishing Co., 1994], p. 258

39. Elijah Muhammad, *Message to the Blackman in America,* [Chicago: Muhammad's Temple No. 2], p. 6

40. Elijah Muhammad, The *Fall of America,* p. 236, as reprinted in "The Mother Plane," The *Final Call* 15, no. 25 [July 16, 1996]: 19

41. Elijah Muhammad, Message to the Blackman, p. 17

42. Elijah Muhammad, *Message to the Blackman,* p. 5

43. Ibid., p. 3

44. Elijah Muhammad, *Message to the Blackman,* p. 42

45. Tape of Louis Farrakhan, Dec. 9, 1990, Compton, Calif.

46. Elijah Muhammad, *Message to the Blackman,* p. 51

47. Ibid., p. 23

48. Ibid., p. 11

49. Elijah Muhammad, *Message to the Blackman*, p. 87

50. Ibid., p. 89

51. Ibid., p. 90

52. *Final Call* [July 16, 1996]: 39

53. Elijah Muhammad, *The Fall of America*, p. 236, as reprinted in The *Final Call* [July 16, 1996]: 19

54. Elijah Muhammad, *Message to the Blackman*, p. 22

55. see *Washington Post* [September 18, 1995]: D3

56. *Tape of Farrakhan*, July 13, 1986, Chicago, Ill.

57. http://www.jewfaq.org/mashiach.htm

58. Mather and Nichols, 1993, p. 186

59. McDowell and Stewart, 1983, p. 65

60. Mather and Nichols, 1993, p. 189

61. McDowell and Stewart, 1983, p. 74

62. Boa, 1990, p. 92

63. Ibid, p. 67

64. Mather and Nichols, 1993, p. 191

65. Mather and Nichols, 1993, p. 193

66. Boa, 1990, p. 92

67. Mather and Nichols, 1993, p. 194

68. Ibid.

69. Ibid., p. 195

70. Mather and Nichols, 1993, p. 193

71. McDowell and Stewart, 1983, p. 69

72. Boa, 1990, p. 89

73. Ibid.

74. Gilmore, M. (2003). Anton Szandor LaVey. Retrieved from http://www.churchofsatan.com/history-anton-szandor-lavey.php

75. Wright, L. (2013). *Going clear: Scientology, Hollywood, and the prison of belief* (page. 560). Publisher: Vintage Books; 1st Edition.

76. Roe v. Wade (1973), retrieved September 24, 2015, from http://

www.pbs.org/wnet/supremecourt/rights/landmark_roe.html

77. Ibid.

78. Fact Sheet, Induced Abortion in the United States, July 2014. Retrieved September 24, 2015, from https://www.guttmacher.org/pubs/fb_induced_abortion.html

79. Ibid.

80. Ibid.

81. Abortion, dictionary.com

82. George Will. (July 31, 2010), "Barbara Boxer's Position on Abortion", Retrieved September 24, 2015, from http://www.newsweek.com/george-will-barbara-boxers-position-abortion-74293

83. Edward Galton, Retrieved October 23, 2015, from http://www.biography.com/people/francis-galton-9305647#exploration-and-accomplishments.

84. Alison Bashford, Philippa Levine (2010). The Oxford Handbook of the History of Eugenics. Oxford University Press. p. 327.

85. Lynn 2001. *Part III. The Implementation of Classical Eugenics* pp. 182–185.

86. Margaret Sanger. Retrieved October 23, 2015, from http://www.biography.com/people/margaret-sanger-9471186#sex-education-pioneer.

87. Ibid.

88. Abortion Surveillance – United States. November 28, 2014. Retrieved October 23, 2015, from http://www.cdc.gov/mmwr/preview/mmwrhtml/ss6311a1.htm?s_cid=ss6311a1_w

89. Finer, L. and Henshaw, S. (2003). Abortion Incidence and Services in the United States in 2000. *Perspectives on Sexual Health and Reproduction.* 35(1). Retrieved October 23, 2015, from **http://www.guttmacher.org/pubs/journals/3500603.html**

90. Lee, M. (August 12, 2015). For Planned Parenthood abortion

stats, '3 percent' and '94 percent' are both misleading. Washington Post. Retrieved October 23, 2015, from **https:// www.washingtonpost.com/news/fact-checker/ wp/2015/08/12/for-planned-parenthood-abortion-stats-3-percent-and-94-percent-are-both-misleading/**.

91. Fontaine, M. (2013). America has an Incest Problem. The Atlantic, January 24, 2013, retrieved October 25, 2015, from http://www.theatlantic.com/national/archive/2013/01/america-has-an-incest-problem/272459/

92. Ibid.

93. McClinton, T., and Hawkins, R. (2009). Biblical Counseling. Baker Books: Grand Rapids, MI.

94. Pedophilia. Retrieved October 23, 2015, from www.psychologytoday.com/conditions/pedophilia.

95. Geisler, N. (2010). Christian Ethics (2nd Ed.). Baker Academic: Grand Rapids, MI. p. 264.

96. Centers for Disease Control Lesbian Gay Bisexual and Transgender Population Statistics. Retrieved October 22, 2015, from www.cdc.gov/hiv/group/msm/index.html.

97. Centers for Disease Control National Health Statistics Report 2013. Retrieved October 22, 2015, from www.cdc.gov/nchs/data/nhsr/nhsr077.pdf

98. Ibid.

99. Masci, D. and Lipka, M. (July 2, 2015). Where Christian Churches, Other Religions Stand on Gay Marriage. Pew Research Center. Retrieved October 25, 2015, from http://www.pewresearch.org/fact-tank/2015/07/02/where-christian-churches-stand-on-gay-marriage/

100. Black, S. (2013). The Porn Circuit: Understanding Your Brain and Break Porn Habits in 90 Days. Covenant Eyes, Inc. Retrieved

October 22, 2015, from www.covenanteyes.com/science-of-porn-addiction-ebook/

101. Pornography Statistics. Retrieved October 25, 2015, from http://www.familysafemedia.com/pornography_statistics.html

102. http://www.crisisaid.org/ICAPDF/Trafficking/traffickstats.pdf

103. http://www.fbi.gov/stats-services/publications/law-enforcement-bulletin/march_2011/human_sex_trafficking

104. Ibid.

Romans Road

Romans 3:23

"For all have sinned and come short of the glory of God."

Romans 6:23

"For the wages of sin is death; but the gift of God is eternal life through Jesus Christ our Lord."

Romans 5:8

"But God commendeth his love toward us, in that, while we were yet sinners Christ died for us."

Romans 10:9

That if thou shalt confess with thy mouth the Lord Jesus, and shalt believe in thine heart that God hath raised him from the dead, thou shalt be saved.

www.ginoskomedia.com

Romans Road

Romans 3:23

"For all have sinned and come short of the glory of God."

Romans 6:23

"For the wages of sin is death; but the gift of God is eternal life through Jesus Christ our Lord."

Romans 5:8

"But God commendeth his love toward us, in that, while we were yet sinners Christ died for us."

Romans 10:9

That if thou shalt confess with thy mouth the Lord Jesus, and shalt believe in thine heart that God hath raised him from the dead, thou shalt be saved.

www.ginoskomedia.com

Romans Road

Romans 3:23
"For all have sinned and come short of the glory of God."

Romans 6:23
"For the wages of sin is death; but the gift of God is eternal life through Jesus Christ our Lord."

Romans 5:8
"But God commendeth his love toward us, in that, while we were yet sinners Christ died for us."

Romans 10:9
That if thou shalt confess with thy mouth the Lord Jesus, and shalt believe in thine heart that God hath raised him from the dead, thou shalt be saved.

www.ginoskomedia.com

Romans Road

Romans 3:23
"For all have sinned and come short of the glory of God."

Romans 6:23
"For the wages of sin is death; but the gift of God is eternal life through Jesus Christ our Lord."

Romans 5:8
"But God commendeth his love toward us, in that, while we were yet sinners Christ died for us."

Romans 10:9
That if thou shalt confess with thy mouth the Lord Jesus, and shalt believe in thine heart that God hath raised him from the dead, thou shalt be saved.

www.ginoskomedia.com

Romans Road

Romans 3:23

"For all have sinned and come short of the glory of God."

Romans 6:23

"For the wages of sin is death; but the gift of God is eternal life through Jesus Christ our Lord."

Romans 5:8

"But God commendeth his love toward us, in that, while we were yet sinners Christ died for us."

Romans 10:9

That if thou shalt confess with thy mouth the Lord Jesus, and shalt believe in thine heart that God hath raised him from the dead, thou shalt be saved.

www.ginoskomedia.com

Romans Road

Romans 3:23

"For all have sinned and come short of the glory of God."

Romans 6:23

"For the wages of sin is death; but the gift of God is eternal life through Jesus Christ our Lord."

Romans 5:8

"But God commendeth his love toward us, in that, while we were yet sinners Christ died for us."

Romans 10:9

That if thou shalt confess with thy mouth the Lord Jesus, and shalt believe in thine heart that God hath raised him from the dead, thou shalt be saved.

www.ginoskomedia.com

Romans Road

Romans 3:23
"For all have sinned and come short of the glory of God."

Romans 6:23
"For the wages of sin is death; but the gift of God is eternal life through Jesus Christ our Lord."

Romans 5:8
"But God commendeth his love toward us, in that, while we were yet sinners Christ died for us."

Romans 10:9
That if thou shalt confess with thy mouth the Lord Jesus, and shalt believe in thine heart that God hath raised him from the dead, thou shalt be saved.

www.ginoskomedia.com

Romans Road

Romans 3:23
"For all have sinned and come short of the glory of God."

Romans 6:23
"For the wages of sin is death; but the gift of God is eternal life through Jesus Christ our Lord."

Romans 5:8
"But God commendeth his love toward us, in that, while we were yet sinners Christ died for us."

Romans 10:9
That if thou shalt confess with thy mouth the Lord Jesus, and shalt believe in thine heart that God hath raised him from the dead, thou shalt be saved.

www.ginoskomedia.com